P9-ASK-067

Ethical Issues for ESL Faculty
Social Justice in Practice

Ethical Issues for ESL Faculty
Social Justice in Practice

Johnnie Johnson Hafernik
Dorothy S. Messerschmitt
Stephanie Vandrick
University of San Francisco

LAWRENCE ERLBAUM ASSOCIATES, PUBLISHERS
2002 Mahwah, New Jersey London

Lawrence Erlbaum Associates, Inc., Publishers
10 Industrial Avenue
Mahwah, New Jersey 07430

Cover design by Kathryn Houghtaling Lacey

Library of Congress Cataloging-in-Publication Data

Hafernik, Johnnie Johnson.
Ethical issues for ESL faculty : social justice in practice / Johnnie Johnson Hafernik, Dorothy S. Messerschmitt, Stephanie Vandrick.
p. cm.
Includes bibliographical references (p.) and indexes.
ISBN 0-8058-4027-3 (cloth : alk. paper) – ISBN 0-8058-4028-1 (pbk. : alk. paper)
1. English language—Study and teaching—Foreign speakers—Moral and ethical aspects. 2. English teachers—Professional ethics. 3. Social justice. I. Messerschmitt, Dorothy S. II. Vandrick, Stephanie. III. Title.

PE1128.A2 H25 2002
428'.0071—dc21

2002016473

Books published by Lawrence Erlbaum Associates are printed on acid-free paper, and their bindings are chosen for strength and durability.

Printed in the United States of America
10 9 8 7 6 5 4 3 2 1

To my mother, Lennie Mae Johnson, who by example taught me the meaning of fairness and compassion for others.

—J. J. H.

To my mother, Lillian Entz Seegers, my husband David, and my daughter, Laura, three very important people in my life.

—D. S. M.

To my parents, John and Norrie Vandrick, who are the kindest, most ethical, and most caring people I know.

—S. V.

Contents

Preface

The seed for this book began several years ago. We were discussing TESL methodology courses in M.A. TESL and certificate programs and noted that methodology books and articles seldom touch on problematic issues that ESL faculty often encounter in the classroom. For example:

1. What does one say when a student asks for personal advice? A student is having trouble with her dorm roommate; a student is seriously depressed; a student is getting obscene phone calls.
2. What does one do about students' cheating?
3. What does one do if a student brings one an expensive gift?
4. Is it appropriate to accept money to tutor a student enrolled in one's class?
5. What does one do when students make racist, sexist, or homophobic comments in class?

As we began thinking and talking about this subject, we encountered examples and heard stories from colleagues. We realized that most of these examples touched on issues of ethics and social justice (just and equitable treatment of all human beings). Many had no clear answers. There was not one "right" thing to do: The situations and issues fell into gray areas and many variables came into play, culture among them. In fact, we even found that we three often had different opinions about a situation and sometimes our feelings were very strong.

As time went on and our discussions and research continued, we became convinced that these issues were about ethics, ethical practice, and social justice. We also realized that ESL faculty regularly encounter ethical dilemmas, but unlike in professions such as medicine and law, educators receive little formal instruction in ethics. For example, there may be a course in bioethics for those studying health science but few, if any, courses in ethical practice for teachers. In fact, ethical issues may be only briefly discussed in teacher education programs and seldom discussed among ESL faculty.

Educational professional organizations may have explicit codes of ethics (e.g., the National Education Association), whereas others may have statements or guidelines regarding ethical practice (e.g., the Modern Language Association of America, the Linguistics Society of America, the American Educational Research Association). (See Appendix A for a list of useful web sites and publications regarding codes and guidelines.) In international education, NAFSA: Association of International Educators has taken the lead in addressing the issue of ethics. In the early 1980s, NAFSA began work on an Ethics Program and established a Committee on Ethical Practice. The NAFSA Ethics Program consists of a Code of Ethics, Principles for International Educational Exchange, and Procedures for Handling Ethics Related Complaints. NAFSA's Code of Ethics applies to all international educators: those in TESL (ATESL section, administrators and teachers of English as a Second Language) as well as those in Study Abroad, Admissions, Advising, and Community Programming. Several publications, many published by NAFSA, deal with ethics in Intensive English Program (IEP) administration (e.g., ethical recruitment, marketing, and ethics in assessing students' English proficiency and readiness for academic work; see Christison & Stoller, 1997; Coffey & Grace, 1997; Pennington, 1991; Rea-Dickins & Germaine, 1999). Few deal with ethics and the ESL classroom instructor. Teachers of English to Speakers of Other Languages (TESOL) has done much work in K-12 standards and in establishing an accreditation body and procedures for Intensive English Programs (i.e., Commission on English Language Program Accreditation [CEA]). Yet standards and accreditation criteria do not address ethics directly.

Discussions of ethics and social justice seem particularly important for ESL faculty in postsecondary institutions for several reasons. First, the classroom is often a student's first encounter with U.S. culture and the academic community. Students often are unfamiliar with what is appropriate and inappropriate classroom behavior and behavior outside the classroom. They are often confused and overwhelmed by the English language and their new environment. Faculty often must deal not only with the linguistic development of students but must also attend to the whole person and adjustment to life in the United States and to life in an academic community. ESL students often turn to ESL faculty for advice about nonacademic as well as academic matters. A second reason ethics and social justice are important for ESL faculty is that ESL faculty frequently encounter ethical dilemmas inside and outside the classroom. For example, two students in the class dislike each other and trade insults in class. What does one do? Instructors often must make decisions quickly, and the best course of action is not always clear or universally agreed upon. How does one balance short-term and long-term benefits or choices? How does one make these decisions? Often teachers make decisions based on unspoken values or beliefs, often upon ethical systems and a sense of social justice that they have never thought about or articulated. A third reason that ethics and social justice are important for ESL faculty is that ESL students and faculty may not have the same ethical systems and may not see social justice issues in the same way. In fact, colleagues may not be operating from the same ethical systems. What value systems and ethical systems are instructors operating on? Do others share these systems? Other faculty and administrators? International students? Immigrants? Do most of the students share the same value system? For these reasons we believe that it is important to discuss ethical issues, to evaluate their relationship to issues of social justice, to try to understand how and why teachers make certain decisions, and to try to understand the ethical and value systems that students are using. By doing this, ESL professionals are better prepared to deal with ethical dilemmas.

OVERVIEW

In this book we define ethics broadly and attempt to show its relationship to issues of social justice. Ethics includes responsibilities and obligations to students inside and outside the classroom as well as responsibilities and obligations to colleagues, educational institutions, the TESL profession, and society as a whole. We have divided the book into three broad areas: Part I: Inside the Classroom; Part II: Outside the Classroom; and Part II: The Broader Context. Part I presents ethical dilemmas inside the classroom, such as faculty responsibilities, classroom management, cheating, plagiarism, political and social tensions among students, and assessment. Part II addresses ethical dilemmas that occur outside the classroom among students and faculty. Examples include questions about advising, tutoring, and relationships between faculty and students. Part III addresses the broader context of ESL in which faculty and students operate: relationships among colleagues and supervisors, responsibilities to the institutions where we work, and responsibilities to the TESL profession and society as a whole. Readers need not read the chapters in order, as each can stand alone.

This book is not a theoretical treatment of ethics and social justice in ESL, nor are we proposing that ESL faculty teach morals or ethics to students. Rather, this book is designed as a practical introduction to ethical practice for ESL faculty in postsecondary teaching situations in the United States. Although we limit our discussion to such situations, parts of the book may be applicable to EFL or K-12 educational settings as well.

Each chapter begins with several scenarios that highlight issues of ethical practice and social justice. Many ethical dilemmas are common to almost any educator in any teaching situation, but some seem especially important for ESL faculty and others are particular to the ESL situation.

These scenarios are based on realistic situations. We have taken liberties in crafting the scenarios and have elaborated stories and experiences we have had and heard about. No real names of individuals have been used. The scenarios are designed to raise issues of ethical practice and social justice, to spark discussion, and to encourage self-reflection. We have not given resolutions to all scenarios in order to allow readers to analyze multiple facets of the scenarios and to come to their own conclusions. Whereas scenarios for each chapter highlight the most obvious ethical and social justice issues for the topic of the chapter (e.g., curriculum, faculty responsibility, testing), scenarios may raise other issues not directly addressed and may be applicable to discussions in other chapters. We have also included an appendix (Appendix B) with more scenarios to facilitate reflection and discussion.

For each scenario, there is generally not one *right* answer. Kidder (1995), in his book *How Good People Make Tough Choices*, noted that there are ethical choices we make that clearly have a right and a wrong answer. Others are what he terms "the ethics of right versus right," those situations we encounter that do not dictate a clear course of action. Kidder contends that "good" people recognize these ethical dilemmas, seek to understand the options, and strive to take the most ethical course of action. Many scenarios here have no clear answers; they fall into Kidder's *the ethics of right versus right* category.

In this book, our goal is to explore ethical issues of the situations, evaluating their relationships with issues of social justice. In this way it is possible to help all of us in the ESL profession to better understand how to deal with ethical dilemmas, to better understand value systems, and to develop tools for making ethical decisions.

ACKNOWLEDGMENTS

We would first like to thank those at the University of San Francisco, as well as those in the wider ESL community, who have helped us make this book a reality. Dean Stanley Nel, College of Arts and Sciences, Dean Paul Warren, and former Associate Dean Robi Woody, School of Education, have provided generous support and encouragement. Two colleagues, Lyn Motai and Bernadette Pedagno, each read the complete manuscript and gave us invaluable suggestions, for which we are most grateful. Many other ESL colleagues have discussed various aspects of the book's topic with us, and in some cases shared their own stories and suggestions; in particular, we want to thank Kevin Cross, Darlene Larson, Penny Larson, Andrew and Gina Macdonald, Patricia Pashby, Mary Reeves, and the members of the NAFSA Committee on Ethical Practice. The students in the University of San Francisco's spring 2001 TESOL Methodology class read and responded thoughtfully to several selected chapters, in a sense field testing the material, for which we are most appreciative. We also received valuable feedback from the audiences at our TESOL, NAFSA, and CATESOL papers and workshops on ethical issues for teachers. And two anonymous reviewers pushed us to rethink and revise our manuscript in ways that have strengthened the book. For his good humor and logistical help, we thank James Barrand in our ESL Program office.

We would especially like to thank Naomi Silverman, our editor at Lawrence Erlbaum Associates, whose interest, encouragement, and professional guidance have been enormously helpful; we have been very fortunate to work with her. We also thank Sondra Guideman, Lori Hawver, and Stacey Mulligan for their assistance in producing the book.

Finally, we are grateful to the loving support we have received from our husbands—John Hafernik, David Messerschmitt, and Jahan Missaghi—and from our daughters—Carolyn Hafernik, Laura Messerschmitt, and Mariam Missaghi.

—J. J. H.
—D. S. M.
—S. V.

CHAPTER

1

Introduction

The field of ethics is a complex one, with roots deep in human history and philosophy. Questions of ethics are complex ones. Philosophers and theologians over the years, from Plato to Kant to Rorty, have struggled with some of the following questions: Do human beings have free will and therefore the ability to choose their actions freely? Do humans make ethical decisions based on morality, or rather on biological and emotional imperatives? Does ethics concern itself with human intentions, or with the actual results of human action? Is the goal of ethics the achievement of individual happiness, or the welfare of humanity in general? Are ethical principles determined by individuals or by societies? Are ethical principles relative, depending on the society and the circumstances? Of particular interest to us is the last question, the question of whether ethical principles and systems are absolute or relative. We explore this question next.

ETHICAL PRINCIPLES AND SYSTEMS: ABSOLUTE OR RELATIVE

Fundamentally, ethics concerns itself with morality, right and wrong. Many philosophers use the terms *ethics* and *morality* interchangeably as we do here. Sterba (1998) described the connection between the two terms as follows: "Ethics is the philosophical study of morality" (p. 1). Ethics can be, but definitely does not have to be, connected to religion. A revered religious leader, the Dalai Lama (1999), asserted that "Religion can help us establish basic ethical principles. Yet we can still talk about ethics and morality without having recourse to religion" (p 27). In fact, the Dalai Lama articulates difficulties with advocating a religious approach to ethical practice. For example, if we tie our understanding of right and wrong to a religion, which religion do we choose? Do we then mean that people who are antireligion, or simply not religious, are immoral? Religious beliefs do not guarantee moral integrity, as history so clearly shows. Much violence, brutality, and destruction have been done in the name of religion.

In addition, ethical systems and decisions are sometimes relative, sometimes changing. In this postmodern age, where formerly widely accepted truths, principles, and standards are continually questioned and problematized, and where even the possibility of absolute truths and principles is under attack, it is harder than ever to know what ethics means and how it applies in one's life. Although we understand the reasons for questioning formerly "absolute" truths, we argue that despite this atmosphere of uncertainty, it is not true or acceptable that "anything goes"; standards and principles still exist and are still important in guiding our behavior. How one determines those standards and principles, and how one determines when and how those standards and principles should be applied, are the major questions we explore throughout this book.

John Fletcher Moulton (cited in Kidder, 1995) struggled with the issue of relativity in ethics, usefully defining ethics as "obedience to the unenforceable" (p. 66). Moulton explains this definition by pointing out that between the domains of law and free choice lies

> a large and important domain in which there rules neither positive law nor absolute freedom. In that domain there is no law which inexorably determines our course of action, and yet we feel that we are not free to choose as we would. . . . It grades from a consciousness of a duty nearly as strong as positive law, to a feeling that the matter is all but a question of personal choice. . . . [I]t is the domain of obedience to the unenforceable. That obedience is the obedience of a man to that which he cannot be forced to obey. He is the enforcer of the law upon himself. (pp. 66–67)

This, then, is the realm of ethics: not the law, not matters of individual preferences, but the middle area where individuals make decisions stemming from their sense of duty, their sense of whether certain behaviors are right or wrong. Note that even the law is not an absolute moral guide, and at times civil disobedience has been the greater ethical choice, as leaders such as Gandhi and Martin Luther King, Jr., have shown.

Kidder (1995) argued against

> ethical relativism that insists that all ethics flows out of, and is bounded by, the situational specifics of a particular case. . . . Carried to an extreme, it in-

> sists that you and I have divergent ethical standards simply because we are individuals. . . . Such a thesis, refusing to acknowledge any common ground of shared values, guts the potential for building consensus. . . . (p. 189)

The many important and complex questions alluded to will certainly not be definitively answered here; in fact, we do not believe that there are always "correct" answers to these questions. The Dalai Lama (1999) warned that

> No one should suppose it could ever be possible to devise a set of rules or laws to provide us with the answer to every ethical dilemma, even if we were to accept religion as the basis of morality. Such a formulaic approach could never hope to capture the richness and diversity of human experience. It would also give grounds for arguing that we are responsible only to the letter of those laws, rather than for our actions. (p. 27)

There are too many variables, including the variables that come with different cultures. But we do believe that there are certain ethical principles that can guide us. Again, the Dalai Lama (1999) gave some guidance about searching for principles; he stated that though we can't set out a specific set of rules,

> establishing binding ethical principles is possible when we take as our starting point the observation that we all desire happiness and wish to avoid suffering. . . . Accordingly, I suggest that one of the things which determines whether an act is ethical or not is its effect on others' experience or expectation of happiness. (p. 28)

Putting the question of ethical principles in an even broader context, Machan (1997) suggested that the focus of ethics can perhaps best be expressed as the question: How should I live?

Giroux (1992), like many scholars writing about critical pedagogy, stated that ethics must always be a central concern in pedagogy. In this book, we explore questions of ethics and pedagogy, along with the many relevant variables, in the context of postsecondary ESL settings. We proceed with the belief that individuals can and do make decisions about ethics, about the morality of their actions. We know that often people have some kind of system of ethics, but would have trouble defining or explaining it, and are not quite sure where their ethical systems came from and how they developed. We believe that the very acts of thinking about, talking about, and reading about ethical issues are helpful.

We also struggle specifically with the question of how much of ethics is universal and how much is specific to one's culture or society. Particularly as teachers working with students and sometimes colleagues from all over the world and from various cultural backgrounds, ESL instructors are frequently faced with dilemmas regarding differing cultural beliefs that have ethical dimensions. Teachers want to respect all cultures, and people from all cultures, yet sometimes they disagree with certain practices or approaches because they involve ethical decisions that they are not comfortable with. Some of the discussion regarding these kinds of cultural–ethical dilemmas has focused on such issues as the treatment of women around the world, and specifically on such practices as domestic violence, genital mutilation, and forced child marriages. A person from one culture who objects to such practices is often told that she has no right to criticize the traditions of another culture. Furthermore, the person herself often questions her own right to make such judgments.

Nussbaum (1999) provided a useful way of thinking through this dilemma. She respects different cultures and understands why people—here she focuses on feminists, especially Western feminists—worry about being insensitive to different cultures and even, perhaps, acting in imperialistic ways toward women elsewhere. But she argues that, regarding human rights,

> an account of the central human capacities and functions, and of the basic human needs and rights, can be given in a fully universal manner, at least at a high level of generality, and that this universal account is what should guide feminist thought and planning. (p. 8)

She also points out that we all understand that any culture has traditions that can be bad as well as good. In addition, she maintains that

> traditions are not monoliths. Any living culture contains plurality and argument; it contains relatively powerful voices, relatively silent voices, and voices that cannot speak at all in the public space. Often some of these voices would speak differently, too, if they had more information or were less frightened—so part of a culture, too, is what its members *would* say if they were freer or more fully informed. When women are at issue, we should be especially skeptical of deferring to the most powerful voices in local tradition . . . that voice is especially likely to be a male voice, and that voice may not be all that attentive to the needs and interest of women. (p. 8)

Thus, Nussbaum argues, critique of cultural practices is part of a natural evolution throughout history. On the question of whether "tradition" should exempt countries or cultures from ensuring basic human rights for women, a recent United Nations (2000) report on the status of women stated approvingly that "there has been worldwide mobilization against harmful traditional practices" (p. 4).

Also helpful in thinking through the role of culture in ethics is the reminder that the very issue of "culture" is now being problematized, and it is important not to essentialize cultures. There is a danger too in stereotyping and simplifying the characteristics of a given culture; no culture is monolithic or static. There is danger too in looking at students mainly through the lens of cultural generalizations rather than seeing them as individuals with multiple and fluid identities and influenced by multiple aspects of those identities. Spack (1997) and Zamel (1997) critique the perpetuating of cultural stereotypes and myths found in some ESL scholarly publications and discussions; Spack stated that

> when we talk about culture, there is a tendency to conflate it with the idea of difference, and thus, again . . . inevitably to identify U.S. culture as the norm from which students are deviating. It is a short step from that position to falling into the trap of developing and perpetuating stereotypes—and ultimately of underestimating students' knowledge and their writing skill. (p. 767)

Further developing this point, Kubota (1999) used the example of Japanese culture to point out that authors of applied linguistics and ESL literature "tend to create a cultural dichotomy between the East and the West, constructing fixed, apolitical, and essentialized cultural representations such as groupism, harmony, and deemphasis on critical thinking and self-expression to depict Japanese culture" (p. 9). Kubota does not argue that there are no cultural differences, but she does argue that "a certain culture is not a monolithic, fixed, neutral, or objective category but rather a dynamic organism that exists in discursive fields in which power is exercised" (p. 11). Teachers' essentializing students, however well-intentioned, may do a real disservice to students of any cultural background.

ETHICS AND SOCIAL JUSTICE

We believe that ethical questions are, very often, also questions of social justice. Thus we place our explorations of ethics in ESL in a context of seeking social justice for students and for all participants in the educational process. In fact, surely a sense of social justice, a feeling of obligation to respect and help others in society, is the most ethical stance possible; it could be argued that social justice provides the underpinning for ethical decisions. What is social justice but an ethical relationship with and toward others? With the increasing prevalence of English as an international language, the work of teaching ESL is by its nature global, and attention should be paid to global issues, including those of social justice. Teaching an international language has ethical implications. For example, when one teaches language, one also introduces others to the dominant culture(s) of that language; thus it is important to convey cultural information without implying that one language or culture is somehow superior to another. Of course students do not have to adopt the culture(s) of the language they are learning, but it is often difficult to separate the two, and may create a confusing and even painful situation for students.

The term *social justice* is sometimes construed to be one used only by political and social activists; it is sometimes associated with *radical* politics. However, we use the term in a broader sense, to describe a way of thinking and acting which can pervade an individual's or a society's attitude toward other people and other cultures. It is not associated with a particular political belief or stance; it can be subscribed to and used as a foundational attitude by people of all political, religious, or social backgrounds.

The connection between ethics and social justice has two distinct dimensions in the context of ESL. The first involves the way classroom participants treat each other: the way students treat students, teachers treat students, students treat teachers, and even the way teachers treat other teachers and colleagues. The second involves teachers' exposing students to social justice issues, and developing their critical thinking skills.

The first major dimension, the way classroom participants treat each other, is critical. It is both an ethical and a social justice issue to set up a classroom atmosphere of mutual respect and tolerance. The classroom should be a place of safety, a place where students can learn without being afraid of being attacked or belittled. This is true in a general sense, as well as in certain specific circumstances. For example, no student should feel vulnerable because of her or his race, ethnic background, religion, gender, ability–disability, or sexual identity. No student should feel vulnerable because of her or his level of knowledge of English; no student should feel shunned or laughed at because she or he is "behind" the other students, or "asks stupid questions," or "doesn't get it," or "holds the class back."

At the same time, a student should neither feel overwhelmed by other students who "take over," nor be penalized because she or he is less comfortable speaking out actively. Teachers need to address these issues, cautioning students against, and guiding them away from, such behavior. A conundrum that teachers often face is how to reconcile students' freedom of speech with other students' rights not to be verbally attacked, and to feel safe in their classrooms. Thus the problem is how to assure these sometimes seemingly mutually exclusive goals. This is a problem that many schools and colleges are facing, as they attempt to allow and promote the free interchange of opinions, yet protect students against hateful and offensive speech, such as racist or anti-Semitic remarks, in class or on campus. There is no easy solution to this problem, but the answer starts with the instructor establishing an atmosphere of respect and support. In addition, the instructor needs to talk about these issues explicitly with the students, early in the semester. If a student does speak disrespectfully or slightingly about another student or her or his characteristics or background, the instructor should gently but firmly make it clear that such remarks are not acceptable. There are ways to express one's ideas and views respectfully, and instructors should help students find and practice these ways. Such discussion can be part of instruction about making and responding to requests, asking for clarification, persuasive writing and speaking, distinguishing between fact and opinion, and other academic skills. It may be useful to take time at the beginning of a new class to set the tone for the remainder of the term. Some teachers, for example, now form a "covenant" with their students at the beginning of the school semester or year, outlining ways in which they will treat each other ethically and with respect. (These ideas are discussed in more detail in subsequent chapters.)

A closely related conundrum is that although students' various cultures should be respected, sometimes it seems that certain values of certain cultures come into conflict with certain universal values which many believe should apply to all people, all cultures. These may include justice to all people, freedom from discrimination, and freedom from violence toward individuals or groups. As noted by Nussbaum earlier, the treatment of women is a case in point. Although it could be argued that the way women are treated in some parts of the world are matters of culture, and that to judge them negatively is ethnocentric or possibly Eurocentric, it could also be argued that there are certain basic human values that transcend cultural divisions, such as protection of children, and protection of one's body and sexuality from violation. These are ethical questions as well as questions of social justice. At the same time, Western teachers need to be careful not to imply that Western values are in general somehow better, more universal. The West itself still has problems in the area of human rights. The French scholar Françoise Lionnet (1995), giving the issues of female genital mutilation as an example, pointed out that

> to condemn excision as a violation of human rights is to presume that such a practice is the only culturally sanctioned form of violence that deserves to be denounced, whereas we know that many other forms of violence are not repressed by law in the Western context, and that some of our own practices are objectionable and shocking to Africans. (p. 160)

Lionnet agrees, as do we, that female genital mutilation must be worked against, through a combination of education and legislation. Her warning reminds Westerners, however, not to be smug since related forms of violence against women and other disempowered groups exist in the West as well.

Thus the question is as follows: How do ESL teachers help students preserve their own cultures and their own voices, yet adapt to Western academic practices and voices well enough to be successful in their education? Or for students taking ESL classes to prepare for the workplace, how do teachers help them preserve those cultures while preparing them to be successful in their careers? This is a difficult and sometimes painful balance for students, some of whom have felt torn between being true to themselves and their cultures, and attempting to acquire the attitudes and practices that will help them to succeed (e.g., in a university or work situation in the United States). Those teaching ESL are in a unique position of being able to guide students regarding this conflict early in their academic careers; this is both an opportunity and a responsibility.

The second of the two dimensions regarding the relationship between ethics and social justice is that of teaching students about social issues of importance. To ignore such questions is nearly impossible, and to ignore them because they are "political" is a political decision in itself. It is true that teachers should not use their classes to indoctrinate students into their own positions on social issues. But to expose students to issues, and to encourage them to think critically and reach their own conclusions, is not indoctrination, and, in fact, is part of the responsibility of a teacher in today's small world, where global issues have become so pressing and affect everyone. In other words, focusing on social justice as a guiding principle does not necessarily mean being political in the sense that one generally thinks of that term. And believing in social justice does not require addressing particular issues; teachers must decide for themselves which issues they feel comfortable addressing in classes. However, it does require at least considering bringing into the classroom some real-life, sometimes difficult, social issues.

Some ESL teachers may feel that their jobs consist of teaching language skills only. But one cannot really teach language in isolation from content, and therefore any decision about the content used in readings, lectures, exercises, tests, and other materials and activities, is significant. Even the decision to choose the blandest of materials is a political decision. Attention to social issues can be woven into the class materials and activities, and can include discussion of literature, current events, and academic and intellectual events on campus and elsewhere. Teaching language skills, academic skills, work skills, and life skills provides the opportunity for students and teachers to learn about problems and issues, and to engage in critical thinking and meaningful discussion and writing. To provide these opportunities for students is a sign of respect for them and their intellects and values, and gives them the tools they need to live in, and make a contribution to, today's world.

A particular way to address social justice issues is to do so by focusing on the problems with stereotypes, and how stereotypes can lead to prejudice and discrimination. Knowledge about various groups will help to counter stereotypes. Specific discussion of the connection between stereotyping and prejudice will be helpful as well.

In order to address both of the major dimensions of the ethics–social justice connection—the way classroom participants treat each other, and exposing students to social justice issues—teachers may find it useful to draw on insights from some of the newer philosophical constructs in the field, including feminist ethics, feminist and critical pedagogies, and the peace education movement.

Feminist ethics emphasizes a "caring" curriculum, involving attention to the needs of the individual, and a cooperative rather than competitive atmosphere in the classroom. (Interestingly, versions of *caring* curricula have appeared throughout the history of ESL, and not necessarily only from women teacher–scholars; see, for example, Moskowitz's (1978) book on "caring and sharing," and Curran's (1972) Counseling/Learning approach.)

Proponents of critical and feminist pedagogies, both in non-ESL and ESL settings, also have much to offer in connection with ethical teaching. Critical and feminist pedagogies strive for positive, nonsexist treatment of all classroom participants and promote collaborative forms of learning. These pedagogies pay attention to issues of power, and attempt to mitigate the consequences of some classroom participants' feeling more powerful and more entitled, and therefore dominating the classroom discourse. Often certain students, because of their gender, language ability, cultural background, class background, race, or sexual identity are effectively silenced, or effectively silence themselves, in the classroom. Ethical teaching attempts to counter this power differential and its consequences, working to protect, empower, and give voice to all students. (See chap. 15 for further discussion of feminist ethics and feminist pedagogies.)

The peace education movement, which is gradually becoming more prominent in ESL as well as in education in general, also addresses some of the same issues. Peace education particularly focuses on modeling and teaching about a broad range of related social justice issues such as racism, sexism, and the environment, as well as issues of war and peace. Peace education also focuses on teaching conflict resolution, both in the classroom and in society. Evidence of increased interest in peace and social justice issues among ESL–EFL practitioners can be found in the recent creation of a caucus titled "TESOLers for Social Responsibility" (TSR) within the TESOL organization. Again, there is a clear connection between peace education, social justice education, and ethical education. Other indications of interest in peace education within language teaching are found in such publications as Birch (1992), Fox (1992), Schäffner and Wenden (1995), and Wenden (1992).

Although few ESL scholars have specifically addressed ethical issues in teaching ESL, Johnston, Juhász, Marken, and Ruiz (1998) reported on their research on moral aspects of teaching in their article, "The ESL Teacher as Moral Agent." Although they distinguish morality from ethics, stating that ethics is "more concerned with accepted codes of behavior" whereas "morality refers rather to internal values, beliefs and standards (p. 162), they address some of the same kinds of questions that in this book we label ethical questions. They also address the social and political aspects of the moral dimension in teaching, and the roles of culture and power relations in morality and moral action, paralleling the connections we make here among ethics, social justice, culture, and power. Further, Johnston (in press) extensively discusses the place of values in English language teaching.

Addressing the social justice aspect of language education, some educators have stated that educators need to be involved in "critical language education," which emphasizes that "language is a factor, like political, economic, and cultural factors, which needs to be investigated in the search for insight into critical social problems" (Wenden, 1995, p. 211). In addition, the current increasing emphasis in public education on "moral education" and "character education" shows that teachers and the public realize the importance of ethical education, and are searching for ways to implement both ethical teaching, and the teaching of ethics. And whether or not teachers use the term *social justice*, when one listens to teachers talking, they often address moral and ethical questions in a social justice context. These issues, regarding the way members of the ESL community treat each other and regarding teaching about social and political topics, are essentially ethical issues. Teaching ethically involves a deep concern for and commitment to people and to issues of social justice. Some of the specific issues may change over time, but the teacher's central goal should always be the promotion of the welfare of the students.

In addressing ethical issues in teaching, we don't want to make readers feel trepidation about teaching, wondering if there are various ethical traps that could trip one up at any point. Although these ethical issues do arise frequently, most teachers are guided quite well by their own ethical systems, along with some thought and perhaps discussion of the issues. Our hope is that this book will enhance that thought and discussion.

PART

I

INSIDE THE CLASSROOM

What goes on inside a classroom? Does anyone other than the participants ever really know? Is teaching a public or a private activity, or both? These questions highlight one of the many paradoxes of teaching. Teaching has both a public and a private dimension. Any classroom is a private, closed space, while it is simultaneously a public stage. For ethical discussion, it is the private side of teaching that is most sensitive, because it is rare for anyone outside of a given classroom to really know what is going on inside. The exact words and behaviors of the classroom cannot be accurately reported or replicated later on. Even participants together within classroom walls often later differ in their accounts of what transpired there. Elementary teachers, for example, often joke about what their young students tell their parents about school at the family dinner table. Their stories may or may not be accurate. Because of the private and very intense nature of a classroom situation, there are few external controls on what happens, making individual teachers' ethical behavior critical. With the power and freedom provided in teaching comes responsibility.

Both students and instructors entering a classroom face a possibly precarious situation and take a risk. One can never be totally sure what expectations are, what will happen, and what the effect of the experience will be. For English as a Second Language students, the situation is even more precarious, because an American classroom is often quite different from a typical classroom in their native land.

We do, however, enter an instructional environment with several assumptions. Students assume that instructors know something that they, the students, do not; that the instructor is able to effectively impart that knowledge; that fellow students have a similar desire for the new knowledge; and that the classroom is a safe place to be, both physically and psychologically. Instructors also assume that they have knowledge or at least a willingness to guide student–teacher exploration into a mutually unknown subject area. They assume that students come to learn, and that the classroom is a safe place to be both physically and psychologically.

If one accepts these assumptions, then it is clear that certain responsibilities also fall on both instructors and students. In a well-run class, both parties accept and carry out these responsibilities. These responsibilities may include establishing and maintaining a climate conducive to learning, demonstrating good will and respect to fellow human beings, and being prepared. Unfortunately, it is not always the case that responsibilities are regularly and systematically carried out. Instructors and students both know that in the domain of classroom instruction, things can and do go wrong. Misunderstandings and mistakes occur. Generally, such problems can be easily rectified. Sometimes, however, solving such problems and difficulties requires a little extra work, some serious reflection, and perhaps even a moment or two of panic.

In this first section of the book we examine the ethical dimensions of several different teaching areas occurring inside the classroom. Some of the areas covered can apply to almost any teaching situation, while others are most relevant to ESL situations. In chapter 2, we look at faculty responsibilities, ranging from simple, straightforward ones such as arriving to class on time and being prepared to more complex ones such as our responsibility to prepare ESL students for the realities of the U.S. classroom while at the same time respecting their own educational histories and practices. Chapter 3 looks at issues of classroom management. Although this volume is mainly directed at the postsecondary level, and one could expect issues of management to be less pressing, such is not the case, especially when students from a variety of cultures with differing expectations converge in a single ESL classroom. Strategies for management can be quite important at the post secondary level. Chapter 4 looks at testing, assessment and evaluation—a particularly important area for many international students whose acceptance into programs and institutions often rests on their success at doing well on a standardized English test. We follow with chapter 5 on cheating and plagiarism, an area where cultural differences between students and teachers can lead to confusion and sometimes anger in the classroom. Chapter 6 addresses issues related to the ethical uses of technology in teaching ESL, a growing concern as technology is increasingly prevalent today. Finally, chapter 7 touches on an area that is particularly relevant to the ESL situation: dealing with the students' political realities at home and how they might influence what transpires inside the classroom.

CHAPTER

2

Faculty Responsibilities

Scenario One

At a small intensive English program at a private university, the coordinator of the program, Mr. Laurence, taught regularly and got to know most of the students. He was well liked, and faculty and students generally considered him fair, even when they disagreed with him. He especially enjoyed talking with students, and frequently saw them between classes and in the cafeteria where he often went for coffee. One morning he arrived at the cafeteria later than usual and noticed 10 students from the high intermediate class sitting at a table, enjoying a snack and chatting. He glanced at his watch and realized that their class should have started 20 minutes before. He walked over to the group and asked, "Are you having class in the cafeteria today?" The group was suddenly quiet, but one student spoke up, "Mrs. Walker hasn't arrived, so we decided to have some coffee." "Does this happen often?" he asked. "Well, sometimes," the student replied. Mr. Laurence chatted with the students for a few more minutes and then went to his office. There he sent Mrs. Walker an e-mail asking her to come to his office to discuss how her classes were going.

Scenario Two

Two weeks before the end of the semester, three students from Mr. Mason's high level writing class at the local community college made an appointment to see the chair of the ESL Department, Mrs. Collingwood. The students complained about Mr. Mason's class because he had only given the class two writing assignments the entire semester. They had done little writing in class, and they felt that Mr. Mason was slow in returning their papers. The first paper had been returned 4 weeks after the due date and the second one had not been returned yet. Mrs. Collingwood asked the students if they had already talked to Mr. Mason about this. They said they had, and he told them that with such a huge class, he could not be expected to handle any more work. Mrs. Collingwood assured the students that she would talk to Mr. Mason without using their names.

Scenario Three

Sergei Vronsky, an earnest young man in his late 20s, was in the second semester of his studies in English for Academic Purposes. He was friendly and polite with his classmates, teachers, and other individuals; worked hard in his classes; and made mostly As. He was in the advanced level and was one of the best students in his classes. He conscientiously did his homework and attended class regularly. At the beginning of one of his classes, Miss Lynne was handing back the assigned essay and being friendly with students as she handed each student his or her paper. When she handed back Sergei's paper, she jokingly said, "You didn't make any mistakes; you must have cheated and gotten some help from someone." Sergei simply took his paper and made no reply to the instructor. He was unusually quiet the rest of the class period.

Ethical concerns with regard to classroom teaching are vast and complex and perhaps partly for this reason not sufficiently addressed in conventional educational literature or teacher education programs. In 1982, Scriven pointed out the "virtual absence of courses on ethical problems for the teacher . . . in either the precollege or the college area" (p. 311). Even today, Scriven's observation seems largely true. More recently, Kennedy (1997), in examining the professoriat, noted the disparity between the lack of ethical training for those becoming academics and "the careful attention now given to the development of professional responsibility or the teaching of ethics in other domains of graduate training" such as medicine, law, and business (p. 20). It has become increasingly clear that ethical behavior is extremely important in all areas of education, including ESL. Thus, we explore some of the obligations and responsibilities that faculty have to students inside the classroom. We examine concerns that may apply to any teaching situation but may be of greater importance in ESL. The overriding question here is this: does the ESL classroom have particular ethical concerns that arise from its unique student body? Just what are those issues—issues that may require more emphasis and attention than in other types of classrooms?

ADJUSTMENT TO THE U.S. CLASSROOM

One of the most important obligations for ESL faculty is to realize that international students and immigrants may not be accustomed to the U.S. classroom environment, and that instructors must not only teach the subject matter (English), but also teach and model the culture of the classroom, both its overt and covert patterns of behavior. In the course syllabus and at the beginning of the term, ESL faculty can inform students of expected basic behaviors such as coming to class regularly, arriving to class on time, bringing books and supplies, being prepared for class, submitting assignments on time, and paying attention and participating in class. One cannot assume that ESL students know these basic behaviors. For example, in some countries students stand when the instructor walks into the classroom; others may wear black for exams in their countries; others need not attend class, but simply pass a final exam. None of these behaviors is the norm in the United States. This is not to suggest that U.S. educational practices and cultures are superior to those of other countries. Rather, the goal is simply to assist those students who find themselves continuing their education in the United States.

As well as informing students of basic expectations, faculty need to model these behaviors. Faculty always need to meet their classes for the specified time, beginning and ending punctually, in the designated classroom, unless a prior arrangement has been clearly specified. They need to model coming to class prepared and with the necessary books and supplies. A teacher who is regularly late for class, as in Scenario One, sets a bad example and may even cause students to view their entire program less seriously. Moreover, Mrs. Walker's tardiness means students do not receive the amount of instruction promised. There are situations in which her tardiness is understandable (e.g., a car accident). In any case, when she must be late or absent, she must inform the program administrator so that a substitute can be found. Also troubling is the admission of a student that Mrs. Walker is "sometimes" late to class, indicating that this incidence of tardiness was not an isolated one. They may like Mrs. Walker and feel she is a good teacher, but they clearly know that something is amiss. Thus, they are in an awkward situation themselves as is Mr. Laurence, the program coordinator. The students may not wish to get Mrs. Walker in trouble and Mr. Laurence does not want to coerce students into giving details they are reluctant to divulge. When speaking to Mrs. Walker, Mr. Laurence will need to determine why and how frequently Mrs. Walker is late without implicating the students.

Good modeling also includes returning assignments with useful feedback and in a timely fashion. This behavior shows students the importance of doing assignments with care and on time. In Scenario Two, the instructor may have a legitimate point with regard to class size and corresponding workload. However, although a reduced class size is desirable, students should not be held hostage in order to make it happen. A writing class has an understood expectation–that students will write a good deal and receive timely feedback. This scenario highlights the need for instructors to work for change within their institutions, but, until that happens, they need to utilize other strategies. Mrs. Collingwood should discuss the situation with Mr. Mason in an attempt to find out why he is teaching the way he is. He may have personal problems that contribute to his questionable performance. Although such problems do not excuse his actions, such information would give Mrs. Collingwood a better understanding of his situation. Addressing the academic issues, Mrs. Collingwood must make it clear that the students rightfully have the expectation of getting more writing practice. She can then direct Mr. Mason to appropriate professional reading on composition and suggest he attend conferences and talk with colleagues. In these ways, Mr. Mason may become familiar with various strategies for teaching composition, including those that facilitate frequent student writing but do not require faculty correction of every assignment. For example, many teachers assign short journal entries and respond to the content only. Another strategy is to use peer editing instead of teacher feedback for some drafts.

Just as students have behavioral expectations for faculty, individual faculty may feel that certain student behaviors are important. They should inform students of these, consistently expect these behaviors, and, if appropriate, model them. For example, one faculty member may insist that students raise their hands before speaking, whereas another faculty member may encourage free discussion and not insist on this. One faculty member may require students to type all their homework whereas another one may accept handwritten homework. One faculty member may not allow food or drink in the classroom whereas another may regularly bring in a cup of coffee and allow students to do the same. Clearly, if a faculty member has a rule against eating in class, it is not appropriate for him to bring in his morning coffee. Or, if a faculty member requires all work to be typed, she should not distribute a hand written exam.

A behavior that may seem especially difficult for ESL students is active participation in class. They need to learn this because it may be an expectation in other classes. In U.S. classrooms it is often the norm to ask questions, give opinions, and even respectfully disagree with the instructor. This type of active behavior may be difficult for students, and it must be both consciously taught (e.g., written out on the syllabus) and practiced. Students can learn appropriate ways to introduce their own conflicting opinions such as, "I think you're right about ___, but ___." Even in advanced reading and writing classes, activities such as group work and oral presentations need to be structured in order to help students to become more active, questioning learners. Many ESL students are not familiar with the free flowing discussions often found in U.S. classes and, thus, need instruction and practice in such conversational skills as turn-taking, interrupting, asking for clarification, agreeing, and disagreeing. Group work and informal class discussions provide excellent opportunities to introduce and explicitly teach civility toward others. (These subjects are also examined in chap. 7.)

For faculty to model behaviors of civility, respect, and consideration is important in helping students adopt these practices. Indeed, faculty have the ethical obligation to treat students humanely and fairly, without showing favoritism. This is done in simple ways such as listening to each student carefully, encouraging each student to participate in his or her own way, and not singling students out in front of others for criticism. Scenario Three, in which Miss Lynne jokingly accused Sergei of cheating, exemplifies this point. If Miss Lynne believes Sergei has cheated, she should speak to him privately, asking if he had help and telling him that he needs to do the work by himself. If Miss Lynne is attempting to be humorous, she has erred. Any negative comment, even if intended as a joke, can be hurtful. Humorous intentions are particularly difficult to detect and understand in a new language. This does not mean that there should be no humor in an ESL class. Laughter induces relaxation, which in turn may facilitate language acquisition. However, humor directed at an individual student is risky. There is always the possibility that a student will not understand the joke and will take it personally. In this scenario, if Miss Lynne suspected that she had made Sergei even slightly uncomfortable, she should apologize to him.

TEACHING AND MODELING CIVILITY

Another important responsibility ESL faculty have is teaching speech act behaviors. They are essential for introducing students to what is considered civil and appropriate in student–teacher interactions as well as in student–student interactions. One instructor recounts a student saying to her, “Here’s my homework. You must take it.” In another instance, the same instructor reports that a student was unable to take a test at the scheduled time and said, “I’ll come in on Saturday morning and take it then.” The student seemed unaware that there were no classes on Saturday and that the instructor would not be in. In addition, the student did not realize that it is not up to the student to determine if and when a make-up exam is allowed. Such comments from students, while probably not intended as rude, do, in fact, get interpreted as rude. This is due, in part, to lack of facility with the language, as in the example where the student says, “You must take it.” Here the student seems unaware of appropriate ways to demonstrate deference and politeness. Students need explicit instruction in classroom civility as defined in English speaking countries. Most ESL instructors have learned to forgive mistakes such as the one mentioned earlier. Non-ESL instructors may not, and ESL faculty can help students with such problems before they move out of the ESL program and into other disciplines.

The hidden aspects of classroom culture that these examples illustrate are more difficult to deal with than just linguistic problems. Just what are classroom dynamics, and how do they affect instruction and student–instructor relationships? Vandrick and Messerschmitt (1997–1998) maintain that in any classroom there is an invisible give and take, or a pattern of exchanges, mostly unacknowledged, that underlie classroom interaction. Teachers and students arrive in the classroom with some preconceived understandings. Instructors assume that students will follow certain rules such as paying attention and behaving respectfully. They will follow through on their homework. At the same time, instructors will be prepared, treat all students fairly, and provide them with the information and skills that they need. But what happens when the instructor or student does not follow these unwritten rules? Vandrick and Messerschmitt assert that on some level both parties keep a mental tally and try to maintain a balance.

In some cultures, this concept of a tally is well understood. Ruth Benedict, the eminent scholar on Japan, noted that in Japan there is a "principle of reciprocal exchange. . . . Many interactions between individuals in Japan [are] controlled by requirements to keep emotional 'accounts' in balance" (paraphrased in Schneiderman, 1995, p. 41).

So what happens when a student is perceived as rude or has made several mistakes on the homework? What happens when a student gives a teacher a compliment or regularly erases the board after class? These are the kinds of small interactions that can shape a classroom and its dynamics.

In such situations, it is important to remember that many ESL students come from cultures where maintaining face is extremely important. A reprimand that might be considered normal in an average U.S. classroom might be misconstrued in the ESL classroom, as in Scenario Three. It is probably wise to be overly cautious when a reprimand is called for. Speaking privately to a student after class, rather than in front of the whole class, is almost always the best way.

Another problem area for many ESL students is learning how to show appropriate appreciation for an instructor, since there are many cultural taboos, at least in the United States, about becoming a "teacher's pet." Students can be reminded that there are ways to show appreciation for a teacher in generally acceptable ways. One of the best is to try to participate in class discussion, a key to success, at least in the U.S. classroom.

Thus, instructors need a kind of radar for the overt and covert classroom dynamics that need to be taught to ESL students. In another type classroom, knowledge of classroom expectations might be assumed to be in place. This assumption cannot necessarily be made in an ESL classroom. The students arrive from a variety of cultures, each with its own tradition of what school is and how one behaves while in school. ESL professionals must acknowledge these differences and make sure that students are taught the dominant academic culture which so many of them eventually hope to enter. A caveat is in order here, however: There is always the danger of imposing one's culture on others. It is not the goal to rob students of their own culture by forcing them into a mold that may distort their voices. To the extent possible, teachers must value their students' cultures and heritages, but at the same time realize that, whether by choice or not, these students are now in a new culture and society. ESL instructors are in a good position to help them adjust.

CHAPTER

3

Classroom Management, Inappropriate Comments, and Complaints

Scenario One

Mr. Reynolds, 38, had taught in an intensive English program at an urban university for more than 10 years and was up for a pay raise in a few months. He was a well-liked, well-organized, and innovative teacher who used current events and outside material to supplement his textbooks. He often brought in articles from newspapers and magazines as well as clips from local and national radio and television. Students seemed to appreciate his providing them different contexts to practice the English skills they had been learning. One morning before his 9 o'clock summer school class, he came to the IEP director's office and asked to speak to her. Ms. Harrison, the director, quickly saw that he was upset and feared that he had a personal crisis. She asked Mr. Reynolds to sit down and listened quietly as he relayed his story. Shaking and at times near tears, Mr. Reynolds explained that he had just received a phone call from an irate guardian of one of his students. The caller vehemently and repeatedly criticized him for his choice of reading material and denounced him as an incompetent teacher. The caller refused to give her name or the name of the student on whose behalf she said she was calling. Mr. Reynolds felt that the caller had given him no chance to reply or explain his choices of material. In fact, the caller did not inform Mr. Reynolds of the specific material she found objectionable; however, he guessed it was the magazine article on children who murder other children. Ms. Harrison and Mr. Reynolds talked about possible courses of action. Mr. Reynolds expressed his fear that this complaint might jeopardize his chances for a pay raise. Ms. Harrison tried to allay his fears by saying that one complaint would not keep him from receiving a pay raise but his total record at the university would be reviewed. They agreed upon a course of action that both were comfortable with: Mr. Reynolds would address the issue of choice of material with the class, field any questions, and urge anyone with concerns or questions throughout the term to speak to him privately. They agreed that no mention of the phone call would be made to the students. Visibly calmer though still unnerved, Mr. Reynolds went off to class.

While Mr. Reynolds was in class, Ms. Harrison received a phone call from Dean Janet Kramer stating that a guardian had called the President of the university complaining about Mr. Reynolds and his choice of material. The President had called the Dean and asked her to take care of the problem.

Scenario Two

Lilly Fong was in her second semester at a small college ESL program. She was on academic probation as she had received failing grades in most of her classes the first semester. She seldom attended class and often came in late when she did. Emma Wang was Miss Fong's friend and in the same class. They often went shopping or to movies together. Unlike Lilly, however, Emma was a serious, hard working B student who attended class regularly. One morning in grammar class, Lilly and Emma were sitting near each other. The teacher, Ms. Peters, noticed that Lilly and Emma were passing notes and not paying attention. Ms. Peters asked them to please pay attention and reminded them that it was inappropriate to pass notes during class. Lilly and Emma continued to pass notes. Ms. Peters walked to Lilly's desk and took the note from her. Lilly held tight to the note, trying to pull it out of Ms. Peters' hands, but she was not successful. Then Lilly shouted, "That's mine. You can't take my paper. You have no right to take it." Ms. Peters stood there in disbelief as Lilly continued to shout at her, got up from her desk and stormed out of the room, slamming the door as she left. Trying to regain her composure, Ms. Peters went on with the class, making no comment on Lilly's outburst or departure from class.

Scenario Three

A veteran ESL teacher, Ms.Wollingsworth, enjoyed her evening ESL class at the local adult school. There were 35 students enrolled and most were eager to improve their English. Ms. Wollingsworth taught the only low level class on Monday and Wednesday evening, so she had students with varying English abilities in her class. Like most of her students, Mr. Alex Moldovski was a long-time resident of the United States with a family. He had a wife and four children and worked as a cook in a downtown hotel. He hoped that by improving his English he could get a better job. However, Mr. Moldovski often missed class, seldom came prepared, and couldn't keep up with the other students. When he did come, he either paid little attention or interrupted others, asking questions or making comments that had little to do with the lesson. Around the middle of the term, Ms. Wollingsworth spoke to the director of the program, expressing her intent to tell Mr. Moldovski that he could not attend the class anymore and would have to move to another class. This would mean his changing his schedule as no lower classes were offered at the same time. Ms. Wollingsworth explained that he was not keeping up with the class, was at times disruptive, and, in her opinion, was lazy. She did not wish to have him in her class.

Scenario Four

Koichi Ono, an 18-year-old, was studying full time in an intensive English program at a public urban university while living on campus in the dormitory. Despite his limited English, Koichi especially enjoyed socializing with other college students and he soon made many friends. Socializing with other college students sometimes meant being around alcohol and drugs. As a result, Koichi often stayed up late drinking with friends and then had difficulty getting to his morning classes. He began to use alcohol to get his day going. His IEP teachers noticed he missed class frequently, seldom had his homework prepared, and was inattentive in class. Several of his teachers spoke to him personally about his poor attendance and work. They feared that he stayed out late partying and that he had a drinking problem. Mr. Jones, his grammar teacher, explained the situation to the IEP director and then spoke to Koichi suggesting that he speak to a counselor or attend a support group. Koichi said that he had no problems, but simply had trouble getting up early and would get a new alarm clock. His attendance and class performance, however, did not improve. One afternoon, he arrived 20 minutes late to Mr. Jones' class and had obviously been drinking. He staggered to the back of the room, and in a loud slurred voice apologized for being late. Mr. Jones continued with the lesson, trying not to draw attention to Koichi. Koichi began speaking to Miss Sandy Iwati who was sitting near him. He tried to take her notebook and began paying her compliments on her appearance. Sandy tried to ignore him, but Koichi kept getting louder and other students were becoming uneasy. Mr. Jones calmly asked Koichi to stop bothering Miss Iwati and to step outside with him. Koichi refused, saying that he had come to class to learn English and wanted to be given a grammar lesson. Mr. Jones then firmly asked Koichi to leave class. Again, he refused. Mr. Jones then asked all the students, except Koichi, to leave the class and instructed one of them to go to the IEP office and have someone call the campus police and ask them to come to the classroom. The students, including Sandy, hurriedly left. Koichi stayed.

CLASSROOM MANAGEMENT

Faculty have the ethical obligation to treat students fairly and with respect within and outside the classroom. Entailed in these obligations is ensuring that the classroom is a safe environment, conducive to learning. This means that in the classroom, students must be respectful of others and behave appropriately. Yet students sometimes do behave inappropriately, with their behavior ranging from exhibiting poor study habits, to being rude or inconsiderate, to being disruptive, abusive, and even violent.

One of the most common classroom management issues is dealing with students who come to class unprepared. Unprepared students such as Miss Fong in Scenario Two and Mr. Moldovski in Scenario Three present common situations. If a student seldom does his homework or is doing poorly, certainly the teacher should talk to him privately to understand the situation and see what can be done to help. The class may be too difficult for the student, as is perhaps the case with Mr. Moldovski. Sometimes unprepared students skip class, leading to their getting further behind. A student doesn't do the homework, comes to class and feels lost, skips more classes, and gets more lost. As with Miss Fong, the student may then act out in class. The teacher needs to explain this cycle to the student and help find a way to break it. For example, the student may not understand the assignments, may have personal problems, or simply may not want to study English. Perhaps the student can work with other students outside of class for a few days to catch up, or go to a tutoring center. Ideally, the teacher and the student will devise a plan for improving the situation. The teacher must, however, be clear and direct about the consequences of the student's failure to improve attendance and study habits. Sometimes poor attendance and not being prepared are symptoms of more serious problems such as adjustment difficulties (e.g., culture shock, economic problems, family difficulties), substance abuse, or psychological problems. If a teacher suspects such serious problems, she should refer the student to an appropriate professional (e.g., a counselor or health professional). In both Scenario Two and Scenario Three the faculty should attempt to discover the underlying problems for the behavior of Miss Fong and Mr. Moldovski.

Even students with relatively minor behavior problems, such as poor attendance and poor study habits, affect other students and the classroom atmosphere. A student who doesn't do the homework, doesn't bring books and supplies to class, and is unprepared cannot contribute to class discussion or group work and may ask questions that were answered during the missed class periods, in the textbook, or in the homework. Such students also dilute the seriousness of other students and the class, as Miss Fong clearly does in Scenario Two. The instructor should not take class time to go over material that the other students have completed and have understood. If other students are confused about a certain point that has been covered, then the instructor may decide to review it quickly for all the students. The instructor should spend time outside of class explaining what the student has missed, but the amount of time depends on the specific situation. Also students need to understand that they are responsible for bringing their textbooks and supplies to class, for doing the homework, and for keeping up in class.

Not bringing required work to class, such as a draft of an essay for in-class peer editing, affects other students directly and may disrupt an instructor's plans. Certainly, teachers need to speak to such students privately and impress upon them the importance of the required work. Additionally, rules regarding late papers and being unprepared for class should be clearly explained at the beginning of the semester in the syllabus and in teacher explanations. A faculty member may choose not to accept late papers, and in the case of peer editing, may wish to give each student a grade for peer editing, with a failing grade reserved for those students who do not have a paper. Other faculty may wish to mark down the final grade on the essay for failure to have a draft on editing days or if there is a grade for participation in the class, lower that grade.

The educational setting, the goals of the class, and the student population determine the material covered, the work expectations, and the strictness of the teacher. For example, students in an adult education class cannot be expected to do as much homework as those in a university ESL program. Generally, immigrants have work and family obligations that restrict the amount of time they have to attend class and to study, whereas international students generally have only the obligation of being students. Additionally, individuals in adult education classes have varying degrees of literacy and education in their native languages, unlike international students, who generally have received a good education in their countries before coming to the United States. Students in adult education classes may not receive letter grades and there may be open enrollment, with individuals joining the classes at any time. Faculty must take all these considerations into account when deciding how to organize, conduct, and manage a class. The most important points are for faculty to convey their expectations to students clearly and within reason to hold all students to the same standards.

Even when a program and faculty are clear about expectations, disruptive behavior occurs. Such behavior may be minor but still needs to be addressed. Just as in non-ESL settings, disruptive behavior is, perhaps, a less common experience but a far more destabilizing classroom management issue than students' absences or underpreparation. Ideally, disruptive situations can be handled by speaking to a student individually, not reprimanding an individual in front of the class; however, in any case, disruptive behavior must be stopped. Getting students to stop talking during their classmates' presentations may be as simple as separating those who are talking and making a request to the class to be respectful of others. Faculty may need to talk to repeat offenders after class, explaining how rude and disruptive their behaviors are. Ideally, at the beginning of the term, students are informed of certain rules of classroom behavior (e.g., be respectful of others, do not use profanity) and language lessons have covered such topics as how to agree, disagree, and give one's opinion.

Yet even with all this groundwork, faculty may encounter more seriously disruptive and abusive students. For example, a student may burst out with a statement criticizing the teacher during the middle of class (e.g., "This exercise is a waste of time. Why are we doing it?") or a statement directed at another student (e.g., "That is a really stupid idea! You must be crazy."). When criticism is directed at the teacher during class, and outside of class, the teacher should try to remain calm and not be defensive. If the student questions the usefulness of an exercise, the faculty member can quickly explain why it is being done and move on, offering to discuss the issue at more length with the student after class. It is best to take as little class time as possible addressing the concern of one student, whether it be responding to a criticism or answering a particular question. It is wise, and often takes skill, not to get sidetracked by one persistent student. An instructor should ask himself or herself the question, "How many of the students are interested in this point or need this information?" If the answer is "few, or only one," it is best to move on as quickly as possible.

What of students who direct hurtful comments to other students? The teacher can remind them to be respectful and considerate of others and offer suggestions about how the statement could be made politely. The teacher should also strongly point out that all opinions are welcome and none will be considered stupid, and no individual considered crazy. Sometimes, however, it is difficult to assess a remark as inconsiderate or hurtful at the time it is made. Often, it is a few minutes after the remark has been uttered or even after class has ended that an instructor realizes the possible negative effect the remark may have. It is appropriate to take time later in the same class period or in the next class period to return to the issue for discussion and clarification. When deciding how to proceed, faculty have to take into consideration class dynamics and the severity of the comments and students' reactions.

Seldom are students violent or potentially violent in class as is Mr. Ono in Scenario Four. When such situations do occur, the atmosphere is extremely tense and faculty must act quickly, almost instinctively, and remain calm. Mr. Ono was disrupting class, was bothering Miss Iwati, and was potentially a danger to her and others. If a student is violent or unpredictable, the primary concern of the faculty member must be the safety of the other students. This may mean getting everyone away from the violent student as quickly as possible, sending for help from the office or campus police, or both.

Faculty have obligations, however, that go beyond dealing with a particular classroom incident such as those with Miss Fong or Mr. Ono. Faculty often need to take decisive action after the incident is resolved, and should be familiar with institutional policies and procedures for dealing with student problem behavior. In postsecondary ESL programs, it is appropriate to ask the ESL administrator to speak to a disruptive student if other attempts to modify behavior have failed. It is best for faculty to apprise their supervisors of potentially problematic students and situations for several reasons, even if they feel they are dealing with the problem well. First, the supervisor may be able to offer advice on how to handle the student and the situation. Second, the student may be having trouble in other courses because of a personal situation known only to the administrator. Third, if it is necessary to take disciplinary action against a student, institutions have specific procedures that must be carefully followed. Generally there is a process in place to ensure that students' rights are preserved. For example, an individual faculty member cannot independently decide to refuse to admit a student to class or to expel a student from school. So, Ms. Wollingsworth in Scenario Three cannot unilaterally remove Mr. Moldovski from her class without due cause (e.g., his committing a serious offense or outrageous behavior). She can, however, suggest that he move to another class (i.e., a lower class) but should consult with the director of the program before doing so. Similarly, Ms. Peters in Scenario Two cannot unilaterally refuse to admit Miss Fong back to her class. In postsecondary ESL programs, serious student misconduct must be documented and the student warned of consequences if the behavior persists. There may also be a formal process involving the filing of a complaint and a subsequent hearing. So, in Miss Fong's case, the IEP director could speak to Miss Fong, hear her version of the incident, and inform her that the behavior Ms. Peters recounted was unacceptable and, if similar outbursts occurred in the future, disciplinary action would be taken. The director would also need to have written documentation of the incident and subsequent conversations with Miss Fong. This incident and subsequent conversation could be documented in a letter to Miss Fong that would then go in her file. A final reason to alert administrators to potential and real problems is that administrators appreciate learning about a problematic situation or student from the faculty involved before it escalates to a big problem. Dealing with a problematic situation early may avert later difficulties, lay the groundwork for future action and in extreme cases, avert lawsuits.

INAPPROPRIATE COMMENTS AND COMPLAINTS

Closely related to classroom management issues is how to handle inappropriate comments and complaints. These types of comments typically fall into one of three broad categories: (a) inappropriate comments, often critical; (b) comments that are really excuses; and (c) more serious comments making complaints about a teacher's actions or performance.

Inappropriate comments or ill-phrased comments can usually be dealt with immediately; others, however, may have validity and should not be lightly dismissed. Examples of inappropriate comments or ill-phrased comments include (a) I can't read your handwriting on the blackboard. Can't you write more clearly? (b) You never wear anything but black; don't you have any other clothes? (c) This class is boring. The first comment may be valid, and in response, the teacher can reply that she will try to write more clearly and attempt to do so. The second comment is irrelevant and would be considered rude if spoken by a native speaker who was not a very close friend. It seems best to simply answer the question and perhaps to indicate to the student that such a comment would be considered rude by most Americans. The third comment could be treated in several ways, but it seems best not to simply dismiss it as invalid. How the teacher responds also depends on when and where the statement is made: in class, in the teacher's office, in the hallway between classes. In class, the teacher will probably want to quickly dispense with the comment and move on but may wish to ask the student to explain the comment by using specific examples. This last comment also points out the advantage of telling students why certain activities are being done and how they will benefit.

The second category of comments is best understood as indirect excuses students make for their behavior. In the following example the student is making an excuse for why he is late to class, though it is manifested as a complaint. A student tells his teacher and then the administrator that he cannot get to class at 9 o'clock as the bus he catches regularly arrives at around 9:15. The teacher suggests that he catch an earlier bus that would mean leaving his house at 8:00 instead of 8:30. The student argues that then he would get to school too early, at 8:45. The teacher informs him that if he does not get to class on time, he will be counted late and four lates will count as one absence; frequent absences will lower his grade. When the administrator hears the student's story, she too suggests that he take an earlier bus and clearly states that the teacher can count him late and lower his grade if he does not arrive to class on time. He protests that this rule is unreasonable, that none of the other teachers care if students are late, and that in his country classes never begin so early. The administrator calmly states that what other teachers do is not the issue and that each faculty member can set her own rules; thus he must abide by his teacher's rules if he wishes to get a good grade. This also provides an opportunity for the administrator to emphasize that things may be done differently in the United States than the way they are done in his home country. Other examples of possible excuses that sound like complaints include (a) You give us too much homework. (b) Why do you make us type our papers? That is unreasonable. (c) Your tests are too hard. In all these cases, the student may be having trouble doing the homework, typing her papers, and taking the tests. The teacher should consider the content of the comments, and for example, with the first comment ask the student and others in the class "How long did it take you to do the homework last night?" "What part was difficult for you?" Such information gives the instructor a fuller picture of the situation and she can then ask herself, "Am I giving too much homework? Is the amount I assign reasonable? Are other students in the class having trouble completing all of it?" Depending upon the answers, the teacher may wish to adjust the amount or kind of homework. In any case, the teacher should probably talk with the student about time management and ways to make the assigned work manageable and follow up later to see if the student or students are managing their homework load better.

The final category is complaints. These often stem from classroom policies and treatment of students. Many of these complaints can be resolved with relative ease; some are more serious. If an administrator has been apprised of a problematic situation before hearing the complaint, she has a fuller picture of the situation and is not taken by surprise. In Scenario One, Ms. Harrison was able to respond knowledgeably when the Dean called about the complaint against Mr. Reynolds. Complaints from and actions against students and faculty are strictly confidential. When learning of a problem from a student or guardian, the administrator will, of course, want to get as much information as possible. This generally includes speaking to the concerned teacher, telling her of the nature of the complaint with or without the student's name, depending on the situation. However, if the student or guardian requests that the administrator not divulge the name of the student, she definitely cannot unless a formal complaint is filed. If a formal complaint is filed, though, the faculty member has the right to be informed and becomes involved with the formal process.

Ideally a faculty member and administrator will listen to a student with a comment or complaint patiently, trying to understand her concerns and feelings. The administrator should listen, not make hasty judgments and not speak ill of the faculty member to a student or other individual with a complaint. In Scenario One, the complaint was that the material Mr. Reynolds chose was inappropriate. How can that be determined and by whom? Is material inappropriate if one student finds it disconcerting or objectionable? How can an instructor balance covering important controversial material and not offending any student? Such curricular issues and academic freedom are discussed in chapters 11 and 14. What seems evident is that the faculty member and administrator must make it clear to students what they can and cannot do. Students may question Mr. Reynolds about his choice of material and may even tell him that they do not wish to read or discuss the selection; however, Mr. Reynolds has the obligation to choose appropriate material and this may mean choosing controversial issues that make some students uncomfortable. Also, Miss Fong in Scenario Two complained that Ms. Peters had taken her note. Perhaps Ms. Peters could have taken a less intrusive action; however, she had requested that the two women stop passing notes, and her request had been ignored. Whether or not one agrees that Ms. Peters' actions were optimal given the circumstances, Miss Fong's behavior was rude and Miss Fong is using Ms. Peters' actions as an excuse for her rude behavior. Obviously, this is not appropriate. Miss Fong needs to understand this.

Dealing with inappropriate comments, excuses phrased as complaints, and complaints is never easy. Faculty should remain calm, avoid being defensive, and when possible evaluate the content of the message. When appropriate, faculty can also ask for specific information and examples to get a complete picture. In addition, faculty need to be aware of their institutions' policies regarding disciplining students, the handling of complaints, and confidentiality of records. Faculty also must judge how receptive and helpful their administrator is, but at the same time realize that even with an administrator they wish were more supportive, for one's own protection the administrator should be kept informed of problematic situations. Faculty and administrators cannot prepare for every situation that may arise and often have little time in the classroom to think about the best action to take. Uppermost must be the safety of students and faculty, and the treatment of individuals with humanity and respect.

None of these issues has a simple solution. One such incident may haunt an instructor for an entire semester, but teachers should remember that no one is immune to issues of classroom management and inappropriate comments and complaints, both personal and general. Even the most experienced instructors can be broadsided and hurt by these difficult situations. What we have attempted to do here is lay out some commonsense strategies for dealing with very uncomfortable and ethically sensitive situations.

CHAPTER

4

Testing, Assessment, and Evaluation

Scenario One

Moving from one level to the next at Eastern Community College is based on a combination of class grades, teachers' recommendations, and a standardized exit test. Two students who were friends had the same score on the exit test, but Carla Gonzalez was an A student whereas Ernesto Mendoza was a C student. Carla, the A student, was promoted, but Ernesto, the C student, was not. Ernesto complained. The director of the school explained to him that for a student with less than the minimum score on the exit test, the decision is made based on the student's academic work during the previous semester. Ernesto did not feel that this was fair, and asked exactly what the difference was between him and Carla.

Scenario Two

In his ESL class, at the beginning of every new session, the instructor, Mr. Souza, distributed and carefully explained his syllabus, which detailed class policies. One policy was that no make-up tests would be given. A student named Vic Chinh missed a test and asked Mr. Souza if he could make it up; Mr. Souza said that that was not possible, especially since Vic had not attended class the day of the test, and had not notified the teacher beforehand of his absence or of any reason for missing the test. Vic was upset, and argued with his teacher, but his teacher didn't change his mind. Then Vic complained about this policy, and about his teacher, to the program director, Kathleen Boiler. The program director was sympathetic, but stated that because that was the class policy, and inasmuch as the class policy had been announced at the beginning of the semester, she supported the teacher. She suggested that Vic talk to Mr. Souza about other options for completing the work or for doing alternate assignments. Vic was not happy with this conversation.

Scenario Three

At Northern University, students who do not have the minimum required TOEFL score upon entering the university are assigned to take noncredit ESL classes until they reach the minimum TOEFL score. Kay Wu, a student who did not "pass" the TOEFL at the end of her first semester of studying ESL, was upset because another student, Charles Chung, whom she felt was less able to use English than she was, passed the test and thus was able to move on to "regular" university courses. Kay, who was very fluent in English and had studied hard and gotten good grades in her ESL classes, felt that the only reason Charles passed the TOEFL was because he spent a good portion of his time taking a "cram" TOEFL preparation course. She felt that he had an unfair advantage over her and other students because he could afford to take such a class.

Scenario Four

At George Washington Adult School, Mrs. Schreiber developed a lengthy test on irregular past tense verbs and administered the test to her intermediate grammar class. The entire class gave the wrong answers to most of the questions and thus failed the test. Mrs. Schreiber was disappointed, but simply recorded the test scores in her gradebook, along with F grades. Two brave students timidly stated that the questions had been confusing. Mrs. Schrieber was sympathetic, but stated that they probably hadn't studied hard enough, and advised the class to study harder before the next test.

Scenario Five

Mr. Barnstein was an instructor whose institution requires that each instructor's class be evaluated by the students in the class at the end of each semester. A standardized faculty evaluation form was used. Many instructors felt some anxiety about these evaluations, as they were used by the administration to make decisions about hiring and scheduling. Mr. Barnstein, despite his efforts to do a good job, had had some poor student evaluations in the past, and therefore was particularly nervous about the evaluations. One recent semester, as he was about to distribute the evaluation form to his students, he half jokingly but half seriously told them that if they did not give him good evaluations, he might not be rehired for the following semester, so they should give him good evaluations. Disregarding the instructions for administering evaluations, Mr. Barnstein also stayed in the room and even walked around the room while students were filling out the evaluation forms.

Part of every teacher's job is testing and assessment of students. Testing is sometimes difficult to do well, and teachers may wonder if they are doing a good job and a fair job of evaluating their students' work. They may also wonder how they should deal with the place of standardized tests such as the TOEFL and to what extent such tests affect the curriculum. In addition, classroom teachers will often themselves be evaluated; what is their role and what are their ethical obligations regarding such evaluation?

STUDENT AND CURRICULAR ISSUES

Most postsecondary and IEP programs require or employ some type of standardized test for admission, placement, and completion of ESL classes. Often this is a worldwide test such as the TOEFL, TOEIC, Cambridge, or Michigan Test. Adult education and community college programs often use exams to determine students' eligibility to move on to a credit program of some kind. Although most teachers have little or no influence over these standardized tests, they do have input into how they are administered and how the results are used. Basic ethical obligations require administering and scoring the tests in strict accordance with the instructions. This is an ethical obligation to the students taking the test, to the organization that produces the test, to the other students taking the same test, and to the institutions using the test scores.

Another ethical obligation is to make it clear to students how the test scores are used. If a test is a high-stakes test, or if there is a strict cut-off score, such that a student may not be able to move to a more advanced level without a certain score, that should be clearly stated. If the decision about moving to a higher level, or to regular university classes, is based on the test score in conjunction with grades in ESL classes, that should be made clear as well. In the case of Ernesto, the C student in Scenario One, he may not have understood the criteria for being promoted to the next higher level. More explanation of the policy at the beginning of the semester and at the time that test results and recommendations were distributed might have cleared up any confusion. On the other hand, Ernesto may simply not like the recommendation. He can certainly ask for clarification of how recommendations about placement are made; however, it would be inappropriate for the director to discuss Carla's or any other student's situation with him.

The larger question about high-stakes testing is, of course, whether such tests are fair, and whether they should be used to make decisions that have such an impact on people's lives. Kohl (1994) and many other educators contend that commonly used standardized tests are written by and for privileged and middle classes, and benefit students in those classes; conversely, such tests are biased against minority groups, those of lower socioeconomic standing, and sometimes against females. Connor-Linton (1995) cautioned that holistic scoring of writing tests may discriminate against L2 writers. Both producers and institutional users of standardized tests should carefully consider the implications of such tests, and testing policies, and look for ways to ameliorate any discrimination caused by such tests and their use.

Yet another ethical issue related to the administration of standardized tests is that of offering test preparation courses. Readers will likely have seen newspaper articles describing the increasing number and popularity of such courses claiming to raise, for example, SAT scores; educators and the public have been debating the usefulness of these courses and the sociopolitical implications of giving tests that wealthier students can afford to prepare for and less wealthy students cannot. A recent exchange of views in the pages of *TESOL Quarterly* focuses on the critical issues as they relate to ESL standardized testing. Hamp-Lyons (1998) raised the issue of whether such classes preparing students for the TOEFL, for example, are educationally defensible or ethical. She states that many of these classes are taught by teachers with no special qualifications in the area of test preparation, and many of the classes and the textbooks used are so specifically aimed at doing well on the test that they are not useful or pedagogically sound in helping students learn and use the English language. In addition, she continued, "there seem to have been no studies of whether TOEFL preparation . . . courses actually do improve scores. . . . Evidence for the effectiveness of test preparation courses more generally seems hard to come by" (pp. 330–331).

Wadden and Hilke (1999), who are coordinators of a TOEFL preparation series and writers of TOEFL preparation materials, take issue with Hamp-Lyons' conclusions. They stated they were also not able to find studies supporting the effectiveness of TOEFL preparation classes and materials, but that "ETS's own research suggests (albeit inconclusively) that practice improves performance" and that their own research in progress in Japan suggests that TOEFL preparation can "decisively raise scores" (p. 267). Hamp-Lyons (1999) replied by making a distinction between

> test preparation that enables test takers to approach the test with a clear understanding of its structure, rules, and response requirements, on the one

> hand, and test preparation that comprises practice on imitated forms or old copies of the test without teaching the language in use. The former is both ethical and essential; the latter is educationally unsound, and the more closely the material approximates to the actual test, the more reason there is to question its ethicality. (p. 271)

Hamp-Lyons is further concerned that test preparation materials and classes, with still unproven value, may cause "detrimental effects such as curricular alignment and raising scores beyond the student's actual ability" (pp. 272–273). If Kay, in Scenario Three, is correct that Charles' high score is gained through repeated practice at a TOEFL cram school, then the results may be unfair not only to Kay and other students, but to Charles himself, who may be placed in university courses that he is in fact not ready for.

Taking these issues and views into account, and acknowledging the current paucity of research on the effectiveness of test preparation courses, teachers, as well as program administrators, publishers, and professional organizations, need to consider for themselves whether it is ethical to offer classes focusing solely on preparing for the TOEFL and other standardized English language tests. Do these classes actually help students succeed on tests? Do they help students improve their English abilities more generally? Or are such classes given simply to cater to students' requests for such preparation? Naturally some preparation courses are better than others. In a sense, these are issues not only of ethics but of social justice, as they speak to whether or not students' (perhaps scarce, as in Kay's case) money, time and resources are being spent on classes and endeavors that are truly useful to them. It is to be hoped, in any case, that there will be better and more conclusive research available in the future that will help to guide institutions and instructors and inform their decisions about such test preparation.

The question of test preparation classes also raises the more general question of "teaching to the test," which can be an issue at all levels and in all programs, both in ESL and non-ESL settings, as recent publicity attests. Even in classes that are not specifically labeled as test preparation, is there sometimes too much emphasis on giving the students what they need to pass a standardized test, as opposed to teaching them what they need in the way of English skills, skills that will, for example, prepare them to be successful in their academic work? Can both of these goals be pursued and achieved simultaneously? Teachers are often caught in the middle of this dilemma. Their institutions, and their students, are focused on the standardized test, because that test will determine their admission to an institution, or the number and level of classes they take; therefore, instructors feel some pressure and even obligation to help students clear this hurdle. They may even feel it is unethical not to help students pass this critical, high-stakes test which has such an effect on their futures. However, instructors also realize that sometimes teaching to the test detracts from teaching for language acquisition and academic preparation, and other goals the institution, instructors, and students have for the classes; taking time away from the real purpose of the class could also be considered unethical. Perhaps the best answer is to aim for a balance among these goals. Discussion of these issues with other faculty and administrators can help. Sometimes a program-wide consensus is useful in explaining to students why a particular class is not dedicated to test preparation.

Perhaps in response to some of the foregoing concerns, the Educational Testing Service, at the 2001 TESOL Convention in St. Louis, outlined plans for major revisions of the TOEFL, perhaps the most widely used test for higher education. These revisions may change the test dramatically. The plan is to develop an integrative format, reflecting all four second language skills areas: speaking, listening, reading, and writing. Thus, the goal of the revision is twofold: first, to better reflect the nature of academic language use, and second, to bring the test into better alignment with the integrated, communicative types of instruction found in many ESL classes in the United States today. If this goal is achieved, it may lessen the pressure on instructors to teach to the test, because it will be evident that the test in fact tests what is already being taught in class.

Some of the same ethical questions, and obligations, apply to the use of in-house standardized tests, such as timed essays or other writing tests used for placement or exit from a program. Not following the stated guidelines is unfair to the ESL students as well as to the instructors and other students in the classes into which the ESL students are then placed. Realizing the limitations of relying on test scores or any single measure alone, it is also important to consider that after students have studied at an institution, it is probably fairer to assess their work in a broader way than depending on a one-time test. Many programs have moved toward basing the following semester's placement on a combination of assessment measures such as portfolios, teachers' recommendations, and in-house or other standardized tests. Again, relying exclusively on a single measure raises questions of social justice, in that students with limited resources can be at a real disadvantage if a test score arbitrarily holds them back, causing them to spend more time and money than they can afford.

For the classroom teacher, of more immediate concern than standardized tests are classroom tests and other forms of assessment that are employed in individual classes. One general ethical principle is, again, that students be informed about how they will be evaluated in any given class. Are they given letter grades? Pass–fail grades? They should be told how many tests they will be taking, and what the tests will cover. They should know at least approximately how many papers they will be writing, and how those papers will be graded. For example, will papers be graded mainly on content, or mainly on language and writing skills (e.g., grammar, spelling, organization, support)? If students will be graded on class participation, it should be explained to them how it is defined in the current teacher's class as well as how it might be defined in various classes at the institution they are attending. Other factors affecting grading, such as attendance and completion of homework assignments, should be clearly explained as well. This information should be given to students in written form, such as on a class syllabus; it should also be reinforced by clear and perhaps repeated explanation and even modeling. In Scenario Two, Vic, who felt he should be given a make-up test, could have benefited from a clear and perhaps repeated explanation of the class policy about make-up tests. It also would have been helpful if the teacher had attempted to find out if there had been a legitimate reason for the absence, and if so, had reassured Vic that that reason would be kept in mind when grades were averaged. Or, if there was a legitimate reason for missing the test, the teacher could have offered another option such as an extra-credit essay to partially address the missing test score.

Another principle is that a teacher should be willing to evaluate her own tests and be willing to admit problems and change the tests, and the grades, accordingly. For example, if many students misunderstand a certain test question, the question may be poor. Or if everyone in a class does extremely poorly on a test, as with Mrs. Schrieber's test on irregular verbs in Scenario Four, the teacher may need to accept that the test may not be testing what she wanted it to test. Faculty can use such situations to evaluate the reliability and validity of their tests and to adjust them. Also, when appropriate, faculty can write a new test to retest the students, or adjust students' grades, as Mrs. Schrieber probably should have done. In each such case, instructors need to ask themselves whether they have constructed an appropriate test, and not assume the students are at fault for doing poorly.

Assessment and grading based partially on class participation is a particularly critical point, in that class participation is a culturally constructed concept. Some ESL students come from cultures where speaking up in class, challenging others' views, and engaging in vigorous exchange of opinions are not only often discouraged but also may be considered inappropriate and rude. Thus a teacher who values class participation as it is found and valued in a typical Western university setting needs to explain such expectations very clearly to her students. She may also want to be aware of, and give some "credit" for, more subtle types of behaviors which indicate participation, such as body language indicating interest, and the sharing of opinions in small groups or during office hours or in written work. (See also chapter 15 for a discussion of gender and social class aspects of class participation.)

Another way that teachers are asked to assess students is with recommendation letters, perhaps for admission to a university, or for a scholarship. It is an ethical obligation to be honest in writing such recommendations. It is also ethical to tell a student in advance if one cannot write a positive recommendation, and to give the student the opportunity to change his mind and perhaps ask someone else instead.

EVALUATION OF FACULTY

Many institutions evaluate teachers as well as students. It is an ethical obligation of institutions and administrators to do so fairly, whether it be through strict monitoring of student evaluations, or through administrator class visits, peer class visits, or other methods. Some evaluations (sometimes labeled *formative*) are administered to help teachers improve their teaching; others (sometimes labeled *summative*) are carried out for the purpose of making retention or promotion decisions. Whether such evaluations are made through supervisors' visits and observations, through peer observations, or through students' filling out anonymous forms about their teachers, it should be made clear to teachers what kinds of evaluations are being done, and for which purposes.

Teachers too have obligations, including taking great care in the administration of standardized evaluation instruments such as those filled out by students at most U.S. universities (if the teacher does such administration, as opposed to an outside university staff person administering the instrument). It is critical, ethically, that these be administered exactly as the instructions direct. For example, students need to be told explicitly that the evaluations are anonymous, that teachers will not see the results until after the end of the semester, and that the results will not affect grades in any way. Then this anonymity and the other conditions listed must be strictly preserved. It is also important that teachers not try to influence students in any way, as Mr. Barnstein in Scenario Five did. When he walked around the room, he may very well have made students nervous that he would see their responses, and thus made them afraid to write honest, perhaps critical, judgments. When he said that he might lose his job if students gave him poor evaluations, he was putting unfair pressure on the students, perhaps making them give less than candid answers to the questions on the evaluation form.

Teachers may also be involved in the assessment of other teachers. For example, some programs have peer evaluation. A teacher's class may be visited by other teachers, and observations written up. An ethical dilemma might arise if the observing teacher feels that the observed teacher, and her teaching methods and techniques, have serious deficiencies; the observing teacher may want to help the other teacher and not write negative evaluations, yet may feel it is his or her obligation to be honest on the evaluation forms. In such a case, it may be that the observing teacher can assist the other teacher with advice on improving her teaching techniques, but if a problem with the teaching or class management is serious, it probably should be discussed with the program administrator as well.

Teachers may also be asked to assist in periodic reviews of the program or institution they teach in, either regularly or as part of an outside review such as an accreditation process, or as part of a self-study with the goal of maintaining and improving standards. This may include evaluation of administrators. Again, teachers have an ethical obligation to respond honestly to questions about the program; otherwise the review has very limited validity and use. And because even anonymous evaluations are sometimes not anonymous enough (e.g., there may only be two or three teachers in a given category, so someone could ascertain who made which comments), administrators in turn must ensure that there are no negative consequences for the teachers who evaluate administrators honestly and perhaps negatively.

Testing, assessment, and evaluation add to the complexity of teaching, but are necessary activities for students, faculty, and program success. Each of the numerous topics addressed in this chapter could be expanded into a chapter of its own, as each area of testing, assessment, and evaluation is extremely important in our classrooms and programs. The issues raised here are those about which some educators feel very uneasy, as so much of the future of their students, and sometimes of themselves and their programs, depends on the way these issues are resolved. Each of these important activities—testing, assessment, and evaluation—requires the strictest ethical attention, as each has substantial and important consequences for all concerned.

CHAPTER

5

Cheating and Plagiarism

Scenario One

Ms. Gao Zhu, who taught Advanced ESL Writing, received an essay (assigned for homework) from her student Mr. So that was far better written than anything he had handed in to date. Mr. So was a very young man who did not seem to be very invested in the class, or in learning English; it seemed that he was in his ESL classes only because his parents wanted him to study in the United States, and because his college required that he take ESL classes. In the essay Ms. Zhu was concerned about, an essay on the topic of the place of music in people's lives, the grammar, structure, vocabulary, and tone were all very sophisticated and completely unlike Mr. So's other work. Because his work was generally weak, and because he often handed in late or sloppy assignments, Ms. Zhu was convinced that the essay was not Mr. So's own work. She did not give the essay a grade, but wrote a note on the essay asking Mr. So to speak to her privately about it. He did so; she told him that this essay did not seem like his other writing; he claimed that it was his own. She asked if anyone had helped him write it, or if he had perhaps quoted from a source. She reassured him that it is acceptable to use sources, but that they must be used and cited properly. In order to ascertain Mr. So's grasp of the topic, Ms. Zhu asked him some questions about his topic, his thesis, and the organization of his essay, questions that he should have been able to answer if he had written the essay himself. He was unable to answer these questions, yet he continued to claim that the essay was completely his own work, and he began to act aggrieved and even insulted that his word should be questioned.

Scenario Two

Ulrich Brandel's homework essay seemed to his ESL writing teacher, Ms. Hani, to be copied or, in any case, not his own work. As Ulrich seemed to be a serious student, one who had worked hard in the class, Ms. Hani didn't want to accuse him of plagiarism, but didn't want to ignore the possible problem. She worried about how to approach Ulrich, but finally spoke to him in private, saying that this essay seemed far better than his usual writing, and that she wondered if he had done anything differently while writing the paper. Ulrich replied that his American roommate Jason had helped him with writing the paper, but that he did not see any problem with receiving this kind of help. In fact, Ulrich pointed out, the teacher had encouraged students to go to the Writing Center for help, and to ask peers for feedback on papers. He did not see how his current case was different. Ms. Hani replied that such assistance was acceptable to a point, if the roommate gave general advice, feedback, and perhaps some proofreading, but that the roommate could not be actively involved in the actual writing of the paper. Ulrich seemed confused about this distinction, and unhappy with his teacher's criticism. Ms. Hani also felt unsatisfied with her own ability to explain the boundary between acceptable and unacceptable assistance, and wondered how she could better explain this complex matter to Ulrich and her other students in the future.

Scenario Three

Yasuko Waseda and Kenji Oichi, two students from Osaka, Japan, were classmates who had clearly formed a romantic relationship. They studied together, always sat together in class, and were often seen in the hallway holding hands. They were both interested but average students who had gotten mediocre grades during the semester. The final class exam was an in-class essay on global warming, one of the topics in their content-based writing textbook. The room scheduled for the test was too small for the teacher, Mrs. Sridhar, to have students take alternate seats, and Yasuko and Kenji sat together as usual. When grading the essays later, Mrs. Sridhar observed that large portions of the two essays were identical, word for word. Mrs. Sridhar wasn't sure how to handle this situation, so she took the papers to the director of the ESL program.

Closely related to chapter 4's topics of testing and assessment are those of plagiarism and cheating. Dealing with plagiarism and cheating is a common ethical issue in both ESL and non-ESL classes. The issues may be more complex in ESL settings because there are differences in the way plagiarism and cheating are defined in various countries and cultures. Complicating matters further is the fact that beliefs about these topics are sometimes very deeply felt and even emotionally charged. For example, instructors often feel that their concepts of academic honesty are nonnegotiable, and any challenges to their concepts, any violations of their beliefs, are viewed as extremely serious (Vandrick, Hafernik, & Messerschmitt, 1995).

There is a distinction between plagiarism (generally considered a subset of cheating) and other forms of cheating. Plagiarism involves using sources in written work in ways that are generally considered inappropriate in academe. Plagiarism could include copying passages from a source without use of quotation marks and citation; paraphrasing without use of citation; presenting ideas as original when they are taken from another source; or even handing in a paper which has been wholly written by someone else. Cheating involves such activities as obtaining test questions ahead of time in an illegal or unsanctioned way (e.g., stealing them from the instructor's office); secretly bringing answers to an exam (e.g., written on a "cheat-sheet" or on one's hand); or copying answers from another student's paper, whether by prior arrangement with that student or not.

PLAGIARISM

Regarding both cheating and plagiarism, but perhaps particularly regarding plagiarism, there are degrees; there is ambiguity. For example, most instructors would consider each of the following situations at least somewhat differently: a student's buying a paper from someone else or obtaining it from the Internet; a student's copying a few sentences from several sources without quotation marks or citations; a student's citing a source but not showing how widely he used the source; a student's citing the Internet as a source but not giving a specific website address or other identifying information.

There has been a kind of evolution in the way scholars and teachers in ESL have regarded the issue of cheating, and particularly that of plagiarism; one way to frame or conceptualize this evolution is to look at it as a continuum that can be roughly divided into three stages. In the first stage, it was assumed, with no room for doubt, that these behaviors were always wrong. In the second stage, teachers continued to believe they were wrong, but understood there were cultural reasons that some students didn't share teachers' firm beliefs about the wrongness of cheating. In the third stage (and not all ESL teachers by any means have moved to this stage), teachers still believe they are wrong, but their understanding of the cultural differences has led them to question, at least somewhat, the absolute correctness of their stance on these issues.

The first stage was one with no ambiguity: all forms of unsanctioned assistance on examinations and papers are completely unacceptable and should be punished severely. This is the tradition that Western instructors have been brought up with, and although strict prohibitions against cheating are often breached, there is still a strong sense by most academics that cheating and plagiarism are both unethical, dishonorable, and unacceptable. They are also often regarded as extremely distasteful, causing a situation that is embarrassing and unpleasant for both the instructor and the student to deal with.

The second stage came with the realization that the concepts of cheating and plagiarism simply do not have the same implications in some other cultures as they do in at least the mainstream academic culture in the United States. In this culture, great value is placed on originality and creativity in writing, and writing is regarded as the author's personal possession (Leki, 1992). However, the accompanying requirement is that, at least for academic writing, the author's thoughts and ideas must be supported by references to other writers and scholars in the field. This requires thorough documentation. This ideal writing style in the United States, consisting of the writer's opinion and voice and style, supported by references to the work of others, may seem self-evidently appropriate to U.S. instructors (and often, but not always, to students who are native writers of English in the United States); however, it may seem to be a confusing and unnecessarily restrictive concept to many ESL writers.

ESL instructors have learned that ESL students represent a range of different understandings of ownership of writing. In some cultures, the words of ancient scholars are revered, and it is seen as presumptuous to claim originality, as if one's own ideas were as good as or better than those of established scholars and writers (Leki, 1992). For example, Shen (1989) wrote that as a student in China, he had to refer to experts in his papers because the Communist Party taught that as one individual he should not claim to have original ideas. When he began studying in the United States, he had to learn to find his "voice" (perhaps a somewhat Western term) by assuming another persona, an American self, to write the way U.S. professors wanted students to write. Fox (1994) too wrote of the sometimes wrenching changes in writing style and voice that many international students have to make when studying in the United States. Thus, perhaps, when students are taught that everything must come from the voice of others, they may feel that there is little need for documentation. This may be the case with Mr. So in Scenario One, although he is taking the stance that students often take: deny everything. In the United States, however, because writing requires a combination of original ideas and references to others, it is considered important to clearly mark the borders between the two by using appropriate documentation. For some non-Western (and some Western, for that matter) students, then, different cultural mores regarding ownership of written work, combined with the difficulties of succeeding in an unfamiliar academic system, make it unsurprising that, as Currie (1998) put it, students "are frequently unsure about the rules governing plagiarism and how to avoid it. In such cases, copying reflects less an intentional violation of a cultural code than a survival measure in the face of perceived difficulties or deficiencies" (p. 2).

In the third stage, some scholars (but definitely not all ESL professionals) have posited that ESL teachers need not only to understand the cultural differences surrounding the question of cheating and, in particular, plagiarism, but also to make allowances for and adaptations to teaching situations where these cultural differences surface. Such allowances are advocated in particular for EFL classes in countries where English is not the first language, but also, perhaps to a lesser degree, for ESL classes in the United States and other English-dominant countries. Pennycook (1994), for example, contended that another scholar's "basic premise that plagiarism is clear and objectifiable and can therefore be easily recognized is much more open to question" (p. 277). He also contends (particularly referring to EFL classes outside the United States) that students' deviation from Western norms should not be simply explained by cultural differences and be considered something to be cured by Western values and Western teachers. We should question the whole concept that students should necessarily comply with Western norms on this issue; forcing students to comply in this way may even be considered a kind of "cultural imposition" (p. 278). In a 1996 article, Pennycook further explored issues of ownership of texts, and of "the complex relationships between text, memory, and learning" (p. 201). He pointed out that concepts of ownership of texts have shifted greatly in Western culture, and that it is perhaps hypocritical for Western instructors to demand allegiance by non-Westerners to an ever-changing concept. Perhaps supporting this view, many scholars (e.g., Bloch, 2001) find that the ways in which information and ideas are diffused and exchanged through the Internet have further blurred the lines regarding ownership of texts, intellectual property, and plagiarism.

CHEATING

The issue of cheating, in other forms than plagiarism (e.g., exchanging or copying answers during a test, having a friend or paid acquaintance take one's seat at an exam) has related cultural dimensions as well, and thus presents related ethical dilemmas for ESL faculty. As those in ESL have gained cultural understanding of these issues of cheating as well as those of plagiarism discussed earlier, they have gone through a similar evolution of understanding and have become at least slightly less unambiguously judgmental.

First, ESL faculty have to acknowledge that strong mores regarding cheating are actually frequently compromised by competing mores regarding community and cooperation. In the United States, there is a tradition of individualism; each person is expected to do his or her own work. However, the ideal of individualism is ambiguous, as there is an opposite value placed on civic responsibilities and responsibilities to one's communities (Bellah, Madsen, Sullivan, Swidler, & Tipton, 1985). Current educational practices in the United States highlight this ambiguity. Researchers and educators often recommend cooperative learning, an approach in which students teach each other, and the classroom is no longer "teacher-fronted." Ulrich, in Scenario Two, has clearly absorbed this message, regarding utilizing assistance from teachers, tutors, and friends, when writing papers. The question of how much assistance is too much is a difficult one.

At the time of tests and exams in U.S. classes, however, the cooperative principle suddenly becomes irrelevant. Although studies have shown that up to 75% of native U.S. college students have cheated and generally rationalized the cheating on pragmatic grounds (e.g., Kibler, 1994), anyone caught giving answers to another during an examination may be severely punished, or at least threatened with severe punishment. It seems that the academic world is sending a mixed message. Teachers who are rigid and judgmental of international students who cheat may even, thus, in light of this confusion, be somewhat hypocritical.

Leki (1992) noted one of the relevant cultural differences surrounding the issue of cheating. She says that in many parts of the world, examination results can determine a student's career and future; thus it is accepted that

> friends and relatives have the right to call upon each other for any help they need, and that the call must be answered. Some students feel as much obliged to share exam answers or research papers as they would to share their notes of that day's class or to share their book with a classmate. (p. 53)

It would seem that the close relationship between Yasuko and Kenji, in Scenario Three, and their subsequent sharing of answers on the test, illustrate this way of thinking.

One study of the role of cultural differences in this area was done by Kuehn, Stanwyck and Holland (1990), who studied students' self-reporting of attitudes toward three cheating behaviors found during test taking: using crib notes, copying from someone else, and allowing another person to copy. The subjects included native-born U.S. students, Arabic speakers, and Spanish speakers. Looking at the students' written comments, the researchers came to the following conclusions: "More than any other group, U.S. students categorized all three behaviors as cheating. Arabic and Spanish speakers tended to describe the behaviors as 'dishonest' instead of 'cheating.' No Spanish speakers used the word cheating to describe allowing someone to copy" (p. 316). The authors comment that "What is cheating in one culture may have an entirely different value in another" (p. 317). A student of our acquaintance told us that for students from the Ukraine it is considered right and appropriate to help each other on examinations. "In the U.S., if you ask someone during the exam to help you, you will be considered as a cheater. However, in the Ukraine, you participate in a kind of collective effort, not in a 'fight for yourself' struggle" (Shats, 1994).

Mrs. Sridhar, the teacher in Scenario Three, might find this kind of research useful in better understanding her students' behavior, yet she might not necessarily feel that such cultural factors excuse or make acceptable the copying behavior. Deciding how much to excuse such behavior on the basis of cultural reasons is of course the crux of the problem—both in a general, philosophical way and in a very specific, pragmatic way—for individual teachers.

Adding to the confusion regarding how to treat cheating and plagiarism is the fact that even in traditional non-ESL classrooms, without even considering cultural issues, some scholars in, for example, composition studies in the United States, now believe that the traditional ideas of authorship as proprietorship, autonomy, originality, and even morality are relatively new in the West, are historically arbitrary, and are now brought into doubt by contemporary theory which posits that there is no such thing as true originality and that all writing is in a sense "plagiarism" (Howard, 1995).

Further adding to the confusion is the fact that many professors in various fields are simply bewildered about how to handle cheating and plagiarism in their classrooms, and that many thus have a tendency to turn a blind eye to it rather than actively confront it. A recent article in the *Chronicle of Higher Education* stated that although one survey found that 70% of students had cheated at least once, "Preventing and punishing cheating languish at the bottom of most professors' 'to do' lists—if they make the list at all" (Schneider, 1999, p. A8). Further, the article stated, some professors who have made the effort to punish and report cheating have found that their administrations did not always back them up, and in fact the professors themselves have sometimes been challenged and investigated by their institutions and vilified by students. In addition, some professors felt that no one really wanted to talk about this issue, and that professors who spoke of having the problem of cheating in their classes were concerned that they would be "blamed for their students' ethical violations" and people would think that such an instructor was "not a good-enough teacher to inspire students to behave ethically" (p. A9).

PEDAGOGICAL CONCERNS

The issues of plagiarism and cheating are even more difficult to deal with and to teach about in ESL classes (or any classes that have students from various cultural backgrounds), given the cultural differences already discussed. Instructors have strong feelings about the issue, and even feel somewhat personally betrayed by students' cheating in their classrooms. In fact, teachers' obviously strong feelings may help students understand the importance of this issue and the seriousness of cheating, or at least the seriousness of the way such behaviors are regarded in academic settings in the United States.

Here we do not state where in the three foregoing stages readers "should" locate themselves. We are trying to provide a context for teachers to reflect on their own values and views on the topics of plagiarism and cheating, and to think about ways in which to handle this difficult topic in their own classrooms. In any case, it is advisable to deal with this topic head on, and to speak with one's students about it. It is better for students to learn about the topic early in their academic life in the United States, in the fairly sheltered environment of ESL classes, rather than later in their mainstream school or university classes. Explicit discussion of Western, and other, standards regarding cheating and plagiarism is useful; some textbooks include readings on the topic. Smith (1994), for example, described a unit on cheating, one in which students try to figure out the causes and results of cheating and even develop a class policy on cheating.

There are also practical ways to help prevent cheating and plagiarism. Regarding cheating, some teachers produce several forms of the same test, or have students sit far apart, or have students leave all their bags and notebooks at the front of the room during tests. Regarding plagiarism, some teachers have students do most of their writing in class, so they can see what the students can do without assistance. Others require several stages of writing, from notes to outlines to multiple drafts. Harris (2000) suggested the following strategies for preventing plagiarism, particularly on research papers: make the assignment clear; provide a list of specific topics and require students to choose one of them; change topics from semester to semester; require specific components in the paper (e.g., "the paper must make use of two Internet sources, two printed book sources, two printed journal sources, and one personal interview"); require process steps for the paper; require oral reports based on the papers; have students include an annotated bibliography (pp. 2–3). Harris also lists signs of possible plagiarism: mixed citation styles, lack of references, unusual formatting, off-topic papers, no recent references, and anomalies of diction or style (p. 3). Further, technology now provides teachers with assistance in the form of special search tools (e.g., Findsame) which will identify papers copied from the

Web, and plagiarism detectors (e.g., Plagiarism.com), which will check student papers against a large database and report on similarities (Harris, 2000). These and other suggestions, although they clearly have some "policing" aspects, should primarily be viewed as ways to help students do their own work, taking the focus away from looking for cheating and "catching" students at cheating.

Clearly and very importantly, aside from but intertwined with the ethical and cultural aspects of issues of cheating and plagiarism, there are important pedagogical issues about the purpose(s) of education and about the nature and goals of learning. In addition to teaching students quite explicitly about the academic rules and expectations regarding academic honesty, instructors need to discuss with them ways in which many forms of cheating and plagiarism limit their own learning. Students who do not do their own work will not learn as much content, will not learn critical thinking and research and writing skills, and will not have the satisfaction of doing and completing assignments on their own. Teachers need to look at issues of cheating and plagiarism in the context of education, pedagogy, and learning.

Students do need to know that there may be very negative consequences if they are caught cheating or plagiarizing. Perhaps misunderstandings can be ameliorated by classroom discussion of the cultural differences and the ethical and practical considerations of switching to or adopting the American mode of writing. Many ESL writing texts provide guidance regarding documentation. In any case, no matter what teachers' personal views are, it is unfair and even unethical to neglect this area of instruction if our goal is to prepare students for additional education in the United States.

CHAPTER

6

Technology

Scenario One

Miss Adhiambo, from Nigeria, tested into the high intermediate level ESL class in a small private university to which she had been accepted, pending her successful completion of a one-semester intensive English program. The teacher of the required "English and Technology" class, Mrs. Brink, began the semester with a student survey asking students about their past experience with technological innovations such as e-mail, word processing, and browsing the Net. Miss Adhiambo reported that she had had no experience using technology; most of the other students in the class had much more experience and were quite proficient in using technology, in some cases more so than the teacher.

Scenario Two

Mr. Marvin Coin taught at a large IEP at a major university where his colleagues wrote and developed numerous ESL materials for publication. Occasionally authors would ask the teachers to field-test some of their work prior to publication. Mr. Coin volunteered to test a set of listening comprehension materials with his high intermediate class. To accompany the materials, the author had developed a comprehensive set of audiotapes. When field-testing the materials, Mr. Coin did nothing but play the tapes and ask the students to do the exercises in the workbook. He felt that these materials should be able to stand on their own without any help from the instructor. Students complained to the author that they were bored in Mr. Coin's class because all he did was turn the tape recorder off and on; they felt that he was neglecting his job, and that they were not getting the instruction and guidance that they needed.

Scenario Three

Miss Billingsley was an experienced ESL instructor with a reputation at her community college for being a good and very demanding teacher. She graded strictly compared to some of the other instructors; for example, she consistently lowered grades for late papers. She also required a great deal of work from her students. Strong students enjoyed her classes; weaker students often did not. One day Mr. Jean Rambault, from France, sent an e-mail to his friend and classmate, Pierre, complaining that Miss Billingsley had been unfair and biased in her grading simply because she didn't like him. Pierre agreed, and forwarded the e-mail to the entire class.

Technology, when used well, can be and has been a boon to language teachers and learners. The modern language laboratory provides creative (along with some less creative) and useful ways to enhance language learning. Computers have allowed students to word process their writing, making writing and revision much easier. The Internet offers students many useful resources that can be easily accessed. E-mail provides a channel for a very real and enjoyable way to use the English language to communicate, and improves fluency. Some students have created their own websites, which allows them to create something positive and original in English, and which allows them to emphasize and demonstrate their strengths, rather than focusing on their weaknesses in language.

The TESOL profession has been paying an increasing amount of attention to technology in the past few years; note in particular the special-topic issue of *TESOL Quarterly* (Chapelle, 2000) titled "TESOL in the 21st Century," and focusing mainly on issues, policies, and pedagogies relating to technology, computers, and the Internet.

But along with the advantages just outlined, technology has raised some concerns, including some ethical concerns, which we focus on here. The first two areas of concern relate to students: students' access to technology and students' use of the Internet. The next two areas of concern relate to teachers: teachers' ethical use of technology for teaching and teachers' development of materials.

ACCESS

In this age when computers and computer-related items are so prevalent, and increasingly advanced, it sometimes seems that computers have become a necessity for modern life. Those who have good access to computers tend to take that access for granted. Yet many in the world, even in prosperous Western countries, including the United States, do not have easy access to the world of computing. In fact, in some places in the world, the problem of access is even more basic: "electrical power is erratic or paper scarce" (Murray, 1996, p. 3). In 1999, Internet users ranged from 43% of the population in the United States to 1% in Indonesia (Murray, 2000, p. 411). This uneven access to computing facilities is found in educational settings as much as anywhere, and affects ESL students as well as other students. Some students have their own, state-of-the-art computers, with all the necessary accessories and all the latest software. Others have only old computers or no computers at all. Some with no computers are fortunate enough to have access to computers at their university or school; others depend on libraries and other public places, or have to borrow, scrounge, or make do as they can.

Other students have access to computers but not to training in using them. If they are not able to learn, either because they haven't been in earlier school situations where they learned, or because they cannot afford to take classes or attend workshops in computing, then computers are of little use to them. Still other students have access to computers and to training, but for various social or psychological reasons feel intimidated by computers, and fear that they will not be able to learn how to use them. Reasons for such feelings may stem from being older and feeling that it is too late to learn; being female and having absorbed the idea that computers are more for males; being of low socioeconomic status and feeling that computers are the province of the middle and upper classes; being immigrants and feeling they have enough to learn about (the English language, American culture, and job skills) without trying to figure out how to learn about computing. Regarding gender, the AAUW (1998) found—in general in the United States, not particularly in ESL settings, but the findings may be generalizable—that boys still outnumber girls in computer classes, and that girls tend to take lower level computer classes; "Research shows that girls have developed an appreciably different relationship to technology than boys, and that as a result, technology may exacerbate rather than diminish inequities by gender" (p. 55). (Regarding gender and computing, see also Spender, 1995.) Computer access is also racially impacted; for example, a much smaller proportion of Black and Latino families than of White families have computers in their homes (Murray, 2000). It is clear that the issue of access to technology is closely connected with, and influenced by, matters of gender, class, and race; thus, access is both an issue of social justice and of ethics.

How should teachers view this and respond to this? What kind of help, or allowances, should they offer? Much of the response needs to be institutional: Institutions should, if at all possible, offer at least a basic level of computing facilities that are available to students who do not have their own computers. Teachers can work to provide such facilities. They can also advise students of places where computers are available to the public, such as public libraries and community centers. And teachers need to be sensitive to the fact that some students who do not have access to computers, or to the latest software and good printers and other peripherals, may not be able to bring beautifully produced papers to class, and may not be able to do, for example, PowerPoint presentations in speech classes. Such students should not be penalized. Mrs. Brink, in Scenario One, certainly has an opportunity to help Miss Adhiambo become familiar with and comfortable with the technology, and she should try to do so in a way that the student does not feel embarrassed by the fact that she is behind her fellow students in this area. In fact, the teacher may be able to enlist the help of fellow students, so that the students may help each other; workshopping and peer tutoring work particularly well in lab situations, and the other students who help Ms. Adhiambo with computing skills may learn other skills and information from her in turn.

THE INTERNET

The Internet is a wonderful resource, but it has many potential pitfalls, including ethical pitfalls. First and foremost, perhaps, is the danger of students misusing sources, either intentionally or unintentionally plagiarizing materials easily available on the Web. Whole papers are available there, and students sometimes do not resist the temptation to pass these off as their own. Students have always been able to obtain papers from individuals or companies, but the Internet makes such acquisitions far easier. Even when they do not download a whole paper, students often find chunks of information or ideas on various websites and download and use those chunks as part of their papers. This kind of plagiarism is rampant; computer technology and the Internet simply make it easier now for students to plagiarize. (See chap. 5 for more discussion of such plagiarism, and for information on possible ways to counter it.)

Another problem that students often have with the Internet is not knowing how to properly evaluate sources. They sometimes think that if they find information on the Web, it must be factual. And their still imperfect mastery of the English language compounds the difficulty in discerning nuances in the language and presentation that might give clues as to the accuracy and validity of information and its sources. Students need to be taught to analyze and assess the source of the information, the sponsoring organization, the amount of documentation, and so on. They need to realize that there are often no checks and balances on what people put on the Web, unlike in the case of published works, which generally are screened by peer review or professional editing before they are published (on paper). This is not strictly an ethical problem, yet in some cases it could be. For example, some students believe that "information" (often, in actuality, opinion and propaganda) found on a right-wing or racist website is "fact" and may treat it as such, thus perpetuating dangerous and divisive stereotypes and discrimination.

Another ethical issue related to the Internet, one that has been much in the news in the early 21st century, is that of property rights regarding material on the Web. When is it acceptable to download software, or copyrighted material, from the Net? What about music, as in the case of Napster and other providers of current music? What about downloading and making multiple copies of material, whether printed material or music? These questions should also be discussed with students, although there may not necessarily be definite "right" answers.

Another concern about the Internet is that students may inadvertently find themselves in awkward, difficult, and even dangerous situations when surfing the Net and when entering chat rooms. They may stumble across, inadvertently or by design, pornography sites. They may get into conversations online with predators of various sorts. They may find themselves courted, stalked, or swindled. Although teachers cannot prevent this, and cannot in any case make decisions for adults, they can make students aware of such dangerous possibilities, and give them strategies for avoiding or extricating themselves from unwanted situations or entanglements.

Less dramatic, but still potentially awkward and even harmful, is the possibility that e-mail sent in the heat of the moment might cause problems (whereas a letter would take longer to write, allowing a person to calm down before sending it). Or e-mail that was meant to be for the eyes of the receiver only may be, either intentionally or not, and either innocently or not, forwarded to others not originally intended as receivers. This was the case when Jean's e-mail, in Scenario Three, was meant for one fellow student but got forwarded to the entire class, very likely causing Jean and probably Miss Billingsley embarrassment and trouble.

Students can and should be taught the "etiquette" of e-mail, and further should be taught that some aspects of etiquette refer simply to good manners, whereas others aspects are actually ethical matters. Examples of the first type, those to do with good manners, include not using all capital letters, as this seems like shouting; not forwarding a constant stream of jokes unless one knows that the receiver would welcome them; and not replying to a whole listserv when the reply is actually for an individual on that listserv. Examples of the latter would include quoting someone's e-mail without their permission or, as in Scenario Three, forwarding e-mail to others without permission. However, even the teaching of e-mail etiquette cannot prevent the larger threat to privacy: the fact that hackers, government agencies, employers, and others can and do monitor people's e-mail, often without their knowledge or consent.

Another area worthy of mention in this regard is the fact that the privacy of people's medical, financial, legal, and other records is being increasingly compromised by the computerization of such records. These are ethical issues for the larger society to resolve, but instructors can alert students to the fact that information on computers is not always private, and can give them some strategies to prevent their confidential information from being shared or misused. A teacher may want to develop a lesson on this issue, including such guidelines as not providing one's social security number on the Internet, not giving one's credit card number online unless one is assured of its security, and asking one's physicians and insurance companies about how one's medical records are safeguarded.

TEACHING WITH TECHNOLOGY

Although technology can enhance teaching tremendously, many teachers do not know how to use it well, or they use it as a sort of babysitter. Using technology not to enhance and enrich teaching, but to replace it, is unethical. For example, if a class too often turns into students being told to "work on your own" in the language laboratory or the computer laboratory, this could be unethical. Some of this kind of teaching, when purposeful and well planned and executed, could be good pedagogy, being student-centered rather than teacher-fronted. In some cases, in a lab the teacher can be coach and resource person rather than "running" the class, and this can be a very productive way of learning. But, unfortunately, in some other cases, such setups degenerate into a way for the teacher not to have to prepare or teach very much. Even with older technology, high school and college students have joked for years that teachers who show a lot of movies do so in order not to have to prepare lessons. Other teachers use the language laboratory or the computer laboratory this way. Scenario Two provides an example of a teacher who uses a tape recorder in this way. Students are quick to realize when a teacher is not engaging with the materials and the technology as well as with the students themselves, and they rightly feel cheated and resentful in such cases.

In addition, when teachers (and administrators) choose hardware, software, lab materials, and other technology-related materials for their programs and classes, they need to be careful to choose materials that will genuinely enhance student learning. Sometimes materials that seem very current, very cutting-edge, are upon closer inspection, or upon actual use with students, just old materials dressed up in new technologically flashy clothes, or worse, are inappropriate or inaccurate or time-wasting. Although some teachers feel ill-equipped to make decisions about such materials, it is an ethical obligation to one's students to learn how to do so, or to ensure that other responsible colleagues do so. In any case, language teachers need to think carefully about which elements of language learning can be enhanced by technology and which elements require live interaction with people.

A new twist on this issue is the rise of distance education, in which classes are taught by videoconferencing and through e-mail and other computerized contact. Clearly there are situations in which distance learning is very useful, especially to students who would not otherwise have access to higher learning, for geographical or logistical or other reasons. And some classes offered through distance learning are well planned and executed. But sometimes such classes are offered because of their financial advantages to the institution, and students are not necessarily served well by them. Language teachers may and should be particularly concerned about whether language can be taught well in this way. Do students still get the practice, the individualized instruction, and the communication that they need in order to learn a language? There are few guidelines so far regarding distance learning. One organization that has provided some very useful and ethical guidelines is CATESOL (California Teachers of English to Speakers of Other Languages). Its 13 "characteristics of a good distance learning program for non-native speakers of English" (1995) include the following points about ensuring that such classes are of high quality and meet educators' ethical responsibilities to students:

> ESL specialists must play an integral part in designing ESL distance education courseware, programs and courses. . . . [L]earners must have ample opportunity to interact in English in situations that require authentic, meaningful communication. Learners must have the opportunity to ask questions and to get regular and ongoing feedback on their use of the language from a qualified ESL professional. . . . Distance education instructors must meet the same qualifications for hire as classroom teachers. (p. 1)

Many of the characteristics listed in the CATESOL guidelines apply not only to distance learning but also to all CALL (computer-assisted language learning) settings, as noted by Egbert, Chao, and Hanson-Smith (1999), who list eight similar "conditions" for appropriate and ethical use of CALL.

CREATING MATERIALS

Materials writers, and web designers, also need to consider issues of access. For example, Kelly (2001) reminded those creating online ESL materials to

> [c]onsider those who use less powerful computers, use older browsers and have slow Internet access. There are many people studying English in countries with slow and/or expensive Internet connections, so it is very important to be careful when designing web sites so these learners have access, too. (p. 13)

Teachers also, like students, need to use the Internet ethically and responsibly. They too need to evaluate sources on the Net and to give credit to any sources they use in their class materials or in their publications. And teachers designing websites need to do so ethically. Kelly (2001) reminded website designers to "Maintain integrity. Be professional. Be honest. Deliver what you claim to deliver. If yours is a commercial site, don't pretend otherwise. Be accurate. Check your facts. . . . Don't violate copyright" (p. 13).

We have mentioned our concern about whether distance learning provides proper instruction to students; another concern about distance learning is whether teachers who are asked to develop online courses and other forms of distance learning are treated ethically by their institutions. Are their rights to their own intellectual property (syllabi, course plans and materials, lectures) protected, or are they being exploited by their institutions? There are ethical issues regarding whose time and tangible resources, and whose intellectual resources, are used to develop the material. This situation is more complicated than that of articles and books, even textbooks, written by professors and teachers, which are generally considered to be their own property. But, as Palattella (2001) put it regarding online courses, the

> issue of course ownership is a complicated one. . . . To start with, what is a course? Is it the lecture notes that the professor prepares? Is it the syllabus? The ideas and opinions a professor expresses in class? The books and articles and other resources that made the course possible? The act of teaching itself? (p. 52)

And many factors could influence the decision about whose property a course is. For example, what if a university commissions a faculty member to develop a distance learning class? What if she is given release time from her teaching courseload, or extra money? What if she is not? What if the person hired to do this is a part-time faculty member, and once the work is done, the part-timer is let go, and other people use his course design to teach the class?

Fortunately, there is increasing discussion not only of uses of technology for language learning but also of ethical issues related to such uses of technology. Among other sources of thoughtful discussion of these issues, we recommend the journal *Computers and Composition* (Ablex) and the online journal *Language Learning & Technology* (http://llt.msu.edu). There are several useful books in this area as well (see, e.g., Egbert & Hanson-Smith, 1999; Hawisher & Selfe, 1989, 1999; Murray, 1991, 1995; Pennington, 1996; Taylor & Ward, 1999; Warschauer, 2000). Bromley and Apple (1998) offered useful analyses of the connections among education, technology, and power, with particular attention to gendered and cultural aspects. In any case, ESL educators need to take responsibility for using technology ethically. Murray (1996) reminded language educators to be mindful in the use of technology, always considering "the complex context of language education," and that rather than using technology uncritically, or allowing others to guide the use of technology, "[w]e need to be steering the course of the use of technology in our field" (p. 3).

CHAPTER

7

Students' Social and Political Realities

Scenario One

Juan and Giselda Morales immigrated to the United States from a small village in Chiapas, Mexico 3 years ago. Shortly after their arrival, they were overjoyed by the birth of their son. To facilitate childcare, Juan worked during the day as a mechanic at a garage where he learned some English, and Giselda worked the night shift as a school custodian. She did not learn much English because the building was empty most of the time. Both worked hard, saved, and regularly sent money to their families still in Chiapas. Both were devout Catholics and very active in their parish. When the parish began offering English classes, Juan attended two nights a week. He was one of the best students in the class. After several months, however, his teacher, Mr. Hudson, began to notice a change in Mr. Morales. He was distracted in class, his homework was done carelessly, and he seldom participated. One evening, Mr. Hudson spoke to Mr. Morales in Spanish to see if he could help in any way. Mr. Morales then confided that he was extremely worried about the safety of his and his wife's families in Chiapas, as they were of Mayan descent, and there was fighting in the area. They had not heard from their relatives in several weeks.

Scenario Two

Miss Jones, a young, new graduate from a TESL M.A. program, began working for an adult education program sponsored by the local school district. She was eager to be a good teacher and spent a great deal of time after class with her students. She felt that, for her first teaching assignment, she was doing well, and the students seemed to like her. Attendance was excellent in her class. One of her students, Mrs. Nguyen, was a mature woman, in her 50s. She related that she was a refugee who had escaped from Vietnam in the early 1980s. Her English was fossilized. She could get by when she had to, but hoped to increase her fluency by attending classes. One evening, Miss Jones began to read aloud the first few paragraphs of the reading assignment for the next class. It was about the war in Vietnam from the perspective of a refugee, and Miss Jones assumed she could count on Mrs. Nguyen to participate in class discussion and provide interesting background information about the reading. However, about halfway through the reading, Mrs. Nguyen began to cry and left the room. Miss Jones was stunned.

Scenario Three

Prior to the break-up of the Soviet Union, Soviet Russia dominated Eastern European countries such as Poland, Hungary, and the former Czechoslovakia. One summer, in an intensive English program at a large Eastern university, a group of students from Eastern Europe and Russia on a grant to study in the United States arrived for a special program. The program administrator made the decision to place both groups of students together in the same classes, depending on their levels. The first week of classes seemed to go well. On the Monday morning after the first weekend, to get some conversation started, the instructor, Mrs. Schmitt, asked students what they had done over the weekend. Almost all of them had gone somewhere—New York, Philadelphia, or Washington, DC. However, a woman from Hungary reported that she had stayed home. Not satisfied with that answer, the teacher pushed her a little. She said she stayed home and read in the library. Still not satisfied, the teacher pushed some more. The student said she read "something." "Well, what?" the teacher asked. Finally very quietly she replied, "Solzhenitsyn, I'm very sorry." At that time the author was banned in the Soviet Bloc. The instructor later realized that the student was terrified that there might have been a spy in the class who could have reported her to authorities back home.

Scenario Four

Zhao Li, a 24-year-old chemistry major from Beijing, had never been out of China before and had been at a large land grant university in the United States for only 2 months. Zhao Li was studying in an intensive English program full time in hopes of improving his English so that he could begin his graduate work and be a teaching assistant in the chemistry department the next semester. He was slowly becoming accustomed to life in the United States but was often very homesick. One of his classes was Mr. Appleton's content-based class, focusing on cultural, social, and political issues. One afternoon Zhao visited Mr. Appleton's office. Mr. Appleton greeted him and invited him to sit down. Nervously, Zhao explained that he had read the assigned reading for the following class period, a reading focusing on discrimination against women around the world, with examples from various countries. He focused on a paragraph in the reading about female infanticide in India, China, and elsewhere. He said that he felt uncomfortable discussing this topic in class. He respectfully, but strongly, asked to be excused from attending the next class session. Mr. Appleton honored his request, assigning him another reading to summarize.

During the next class, Mr. Appleton began discussion of the assigned reading. Students were actively participating and listening carefully to each other. Nureldin Abdelgadir, a bright 22-year-old man from Sudan, spoke up passionately regarding the practice of "female circumcision," arguing that Westerners had no right to criticize practices that were part of the culture of another country or region. Mr. Appleton and the other students immediately recognized the depth of his feelings and all fell silent.

ESL instructors may find themselves working in a variety of settings ranging from adult education programs with mainly immigrant and refugee students to community college programs or intensive English programs associated with colleges and universities. Each type of program has a different student body. Some programs work with students who have literacy needs. Others work with relatively privileged international students. Ages can range from teenagers to senior citizens. Some students are at or close to the poverty level whereas others may be very well off financially. Some come from countries torn by strife.

SOCIAL AND ECONOMIC REALITIES

Students' social and political realities come into play in all ESL classrooms and sometimes intersect with each other. Mr. and Mrs. Morales, in Scenario One for example, struggle to make ends meet. At the same time, there is political unrest in their country. Such factors clearly influence academic success. On the other hand, intensive English instructors frequently encounter wealthy students who fly back home first class for every school break.

Ethically, instructors must recognize the challenges each student presents. Sometimes, this recognition manifests itself in a small way, such as selecting an inexpensive textbook for students who do not have much money. Economic and family hardship may make it difficult for students to attend class regularly or to complete work on time. To the extent possible, instructors need to take account of these realities in students' lives and adjust accordingly. This does not mean allowing students to "slide" by, doing very little. But it may mean giving students extra time to complete the work, as well as words of encouragement.

On the other end of the spectrum, privileged students who seem to have everything also provide instructors with challenges. Vandrick (1995a) pointed out that such students come from families of power and influence in their native countries or countries of origin, and often speak of and write about summer homes, expensive vacations, and luxury cars. These students may take their privilege for granted, and not understand the social and political aspects of why some people have wealth and power and others do not. Vandrick urges that educators do what they can "to make small dents in the injustices perpetuated in societal systems in which there is a vast divide between the privileged and the far less privileged" (p. 380). To this end, she suggests that instructors help all students understand how social–political systems allow some people but not others to acquire and maintain power and privilege. For this purpose, as well as for the more general one of promoting understanding and social justice, instructors can set up classroom activities where students encounter a wide range of opinions and where they can conduct a rigorous examination of values, both theirs and others, while learning to disagree respectfully and treat others with civility, despite differences of background and opinion. These kinds of discussions will help all students, privileged or less privileged, to become critical thinkers and responsible world citizens.

POLITICAL REALITIES

In addition to being cognizant of students' social and economic realities, ESL instructors and administrators need to be constantly vigilant regarding any political dynamics that might concern students. New instructors might wish to ask experienced teachers about what issues have caused problems in the past. For example, one teacher reports that during the reign of the Shah of Iran in the 1970s, an Iranian student refused to participate in class discussions, convinced of the possibility that another Iranian student in the class might be a spy planted by the Shah. This situation is similar to Scenario Three, where the Hungarian student feared that the Soviet students might be spying on her. An instructor may never know the true identity of every individual in the class, and, if a student feels threatened by another student from the same country, instructors must take care not to inadvertently place someone in harm's way.

Political realities manifest themselves in two different ways within the classroom. First, current trouble at home can affect an individual student personally, as in the case of Mr. and Mrs. Morales and their concerns for their families in Chiapas. So can memories of past problems, as was the case with Mrs. Nguyen in Scenario Two. These types of problems affect students individually in many ways, some of which may never be revealed to the instructor. In her article on hidden identities of students, Vandrick (1997) noted that, in any teaching situation, there is a lot a teacher may not know about individual students regarding their personal lives, such as their suffering from an illness or an eating disorder, marital discord, sexual identity issues, or concern about strife at home. Any of these may affect academic performance. Concentrating on academic work is difficult in such circumstances. Students may not necessarily relay this information to an instructor. They may not even be aware themselves why they are having trouble concentrating.

In addition to longstanding issues, sometimes students go through a sudden, specific crisis in their lives, perhaps relating to the political situation in their home countries, as in the case of Mr. and Mrs. Morales. In offering advice, Greenblatt (1999) observed, "A crisis produces both personal and social reactions that rattle and shake whatever momentary stasis individuals and groups have reached . . ." (p. 23). He continued, "Some individuals lose sleep, stop eating, become severely agitated, depressed and withdrawn" (pp. 23–24).

Political crises at home are clearly beyond the control of an ESL instructor, yet it is the instructor who must help the student and the class cope. One of the first steps an instructor must take is to assess the situation. This includes keeping up with current events and then remembering that a given event might affect individual students in the class. After class, or at another appropriate time, an instructor can ask a student directly about the situation. A student may or may not wish to discuss the issue. Greenblatt observes, ". . . care has to be taken to assure that barriers of generation, status, and gender are not accidentally built into the mechanism for communication" (p. 24). For example, ". . . women might be quite resistant to sharing their concerns with men when trauma threatens . . ." (p. 24).

In such situations, an instructor should consider bringing in others such as a peer or a counselor. Often, reassurance and information regarding resources are the most an instructor can offer, but for the student, these assurances of care and interest are extremely important. Greenblatt advises, "We need to use all the resources we can muster to relieve anxiety and assure the safety and academic progress of our students . . ." (p. 52). This includes "sensitive listening, advocacy, and sustained emotional support" (p. 52). In Scenario One, Mr. Hudson clearly displayed some of this sensitivity toward Mr. and Mrs. Morales.

In addition, instructors need to be mindful of an individual student's memories of past strife. Sometimes refugees have been traumatized physically, psychologically, or both in their home countries. They may have experienced the loss of loved ones. Thus, they may have difficulty with class discussions when political issues emerge or when answering simple questions about their families, as was the case with Mrs. Nguyen in Scenario Two. In such instances, most ESL instructors avoid discussing past issues and focus on the present and future for their students. Here again, sensitivity and sustained emotional support are essential. In Scenario Two, perhaps with more experience, Miss Jones could have anticipated that Mrs. Nguyen would find the reading emotionally traumatic. She might have talked to Mrs. Nguyen beforehand and given her an alternative library assignment or even skipped the reading entirely.

A second type of political reality that sometimes confronts ESL instructors occurs when students from two conflicted countries find themselves in class with each other. The issues may become overt and heat up in the classroom itself. When this happens, the ethical problems are difficult. The first task is to recognize each student as an individual and not as a representative of his or her government. When unexpected political conflicts surface in the classroom, it is highly unlikely that the instructor can be the ultimate peacemaker. In offering guidance for developing a peaceful classroom, Birch (1993) related the following incident:

> . . . years ago, in Madrid, Spain, a fistfight erupted in my class between a Basque student and a Franco supporter over a seemingly uncontroversial historical point. Their classmates acted quickly to bring the situation under control. . . . The two students ignored each other after that, but their antipathy created a tensely charged classroom atmosphere which interfered with learning. . . . (p. 13)

Birch maintains that ". . . we cannot expect external political and ethnic conflicts to vanish magically within the walls of the peaceful classroom . . ." (p. 13).

What an instructor can remember, however, is that there is usually a power element involved and that the conflict is not among equals. In Scenario Three, for example, clearly the Russian students represented the dominant political force. Therefore, teachers should not knowingly place students in awkward or even possibly dangerous positions. It may be appropriate to deliberately but unobtrusively place students from nations in conflict in different classes or sections before classes begin, or even afterward, if difficulties arise. If this is not a possibility, one can keep such students physically away from each other by seating them on opposite sides of the room and not placing them together in discussion groups with the idealistic notion that they will learn to work out their differences.

Although it may be difficult to keep abreast of every international conflict around the world, it is very important for teachers to monitor current events from a global perspective. Situations change constantly, and the purpose of monitoring is to anticipate, to some extent, where problems might arise. For example, there is continued conflict between Israel and its Arab neighbors. There is still tension between Taiwan and Mainland China, and in the former Yugoslavia. In addition, many Asians still resent the Japanese because of World War Two. Instructors' and administrators' knowledge of potential international hotspots might lead to some pre-emptive decisions as to placement of students before classes begin or simple awareness that certain political issues will need to be treated with care in a given classroom.

Furthermore, to the extent possible, one can work to develop a peaceful classroom conducive to learning, where individuals treat each other with civility and respect. At the beginning of a course, instructors might wish to spend a few minutes of class time to develop a "learning covenant."[1] Students are asked to identify those elements of the classroom environment that they find most conducive to learning. A student recorder is appointed to take notes, which are then given to the instructor who types them up and hands them out in outline form for brief discussion at the start of the next class. During the semester, if problems arise (e.g., one student seems to dominate the discussion), the "covenant" can be reexamined. For example, selected items from a recent covenant developed in a class team taught by Messerschmitt and her colleague Shimabukuro include the need to:

1. Practice open-mindedness so that others may feel the freedom to express themselves, to inquire, to disagree.
2. Strive to verbally participate in order to create a dialogic learning environment which benefits everyone.
3. Appreciate the beauty of our cultural differences and continually attempt to understand these differences.
4. Provide positive feedback when class members engage in risk-taking.
5. Employ active listening skills so that others may feel that their contributions are valued.
6. Interject humor in class interactions.
7. Promote an atmosphere that encourages spontaneity and creativity.

Additional suggestions from Birch (1993) include working with students through role play so that they can learn not to insult, judge, or threaten

[1]The authors wish to acknowledge Gini Shimabukuro for her ideas on developing and implementing the "covenant" activity.

other students. Teachers must also learn to listen actively, even if they do not agree with the speaker. Students must learn positive interdependence such that they deal with each other ". . . out of a sense of security, autonomy, shared knowledge, and shared responsibility" (p. 8).

THE CONVERGENCE OF SOCIAL AND POLITICAL REALITIES

Sometimes it is not clear whether a classroom problem has a social or a political reality at its base. Often the two areas converge and the root causes cannot really be teased apart, as in the case of Scenario Four, in which two students, in different ways, voice their objections to the class content. Unfortunately, Mr. Appleton had two conundrums to face in his class. In the case of Zhao Li, it is not clear if his reaction to the reading on infanticide is based on his personal beliefs or the official policy of his government. It is not necessary for an instructor to make such a determination and, in fact to do so, might involve intrusive probing of a student's private views. Furthermore, if the student's private views conflict with those of the government or other official body, the student may be placing himself at risk if he speaks out. In such instances, it is appropriate to provide alternative assignments to the students. It seems hasty to eliminate the reading selection based on one student's objection as other students may benefit from examining difficult and controversial topics. However, if several students find the material offensive an instructor may wish to modify her lesson plans or eliminate the reading.

Scenario Four also raises the knotty issue of how teachers should address practices that have cultural or religious roots that seem antithetical to human rights. As highlighted in the introduction, teachers must confront the difficult question of how much of ethics is universal and how much is specific to a given culture or society. Teachers want to respect other cultures and their practices, yet may feel that certain universal ethical principles, such as avoiding violence against individuals' bodies, should transcend specific cultural traditions. Many believe that the issues in question in Scenario Four, female infanticide and female genital mutilation, fall in this category.

In the case of Nureldin, Mr. Appleton would ideally acknowledge Nureldin's strong feelings and the need to respect them. Then he could point out that in U.S. academic settings, even when people have very strong points of view, it is nevertheless usual to examine all sides of the issue in a calm, measured way. A situation such as described in Scenario Four provides instructors the opportunity to model and teach debate and ways to respectfully disagree and argue in English.

Scenario Four contrasts two different student reactions to controversial issues, one in which the student asks to be excused from the class and the other in which the student voices strong opinions. Another way in which some students have reacted is to confront the issue and work through it. In a paper responding to a discussion in a TESL methodology class on the issue of dealing with controversial content, Hyun Mee Lee (2001), from Korea, wrote:

> While discussing eating habits of various countries, someone asked me with a smirk, "Koreans eat dogs, don't they?" At that moment, I felt humiliated because I had also personally despised dog eaters in my country and thus I had hoped not to hear this question in the discussion. However, on second thought, I asked myself, "Why should I feel smaller due to the part of both my culture and social practice that used to be done by my ancestors?" Therefore, I explained with confidence, "Yes, it is true that some Koreans still eat dogs, but I don't think Koreans are cruel and primitive for that fact. We have just regarded dogs not as friends but rather as livestock. . . ." Some people in other countries eat cats or monkeys, but I don't think their eating habits are not civilized because I respect our social and cultural differences." I felt everyone seemed to understand my point of view. Moreover, my ESL instructor added that we were all different and it was natural for us to keep our own ways. She said each of us should be very proud of and appreciate our cultures. Her conclusion was good enough to encourage me. (p. 1)

In some respects, it is precisely this international aspect of teaching that makes ESL unique, because teachers cannot ignore the social and political background of the students and its impact on their studies, on their behavior, on the choice of curriculum, and on instruction. Thus, it is appropriate to recognize these influences and take appropriate action within the classroom. Ignoring these realities and hoping that they will never surface in class is unrealistic. Teachers need to be realistic about what can and cannot be done about various situations and then make the best possible decision while striving for a peaceful classroom conducive to language learning.

PART

II

OUTSIDE THE CLASSROOM

Faculty responsibilities toward students do not end when faculty leave the classroom. Faculty have ethical responsibilities toward students that extend beyond the classroom and beyond strictly academic areas. Although the situations inside and outside the classroom may differ, the ethical responsibilities of faculty in both places are similar, differing largely in degree rather than kind. These ethical responsibilities apply to all faculty, but ESL faculty are particularly important for ESL students as sources of social and cultural information as well as academic (English) information.

Although important both inside and outside the classroom, two factors seem especially crucial in interactions between faculty and students outside the classroom: (a) the inherent differences in the power faculty and students have and (b) legal and moral issues of confidentiality.

Faculty are in positions of authority and thus have more power than students. This is not inherently negative, and faculty can use their power to benefit students. The roles of, and the respect given to, faculty vary from culture to culture. So ESL students from different cultures and countries may come to class with expectations of teachers that differ from those of students in the United States as well as from those of other students in the class. Ideas about what constitutes a good student may differ as well. In general, however, ESL students view teachers as respected authorities who impart knowledge, and they take teachers' instructions and advice very seriously. Students may not be used to questioning faculty or offering opinions that differ from their teachers', and they may not be used to faculty taking an interest in them outside of class. For example, suggestions made by a teacher may be viewed as commands instead of mere suggestions. An invitation to a party by a teacher may be seen as one a student cannot refuse. Students may feel that if they do not agree with the teacher or do not do what he or she says, their grades will be lowered. Faculty need to use their power wisely and above all be cognizant of the power differential and how their words and actions may be interpreted by students.

The second factor that is especially important outside as well as inside the classroom is confidentiality. Legally certain information about students cannot be given to anyone except the student without the student's permission, except in situations where the student is in danger or if other individuals are placed in danger. The Family Educational Rights and Privacy Act grants college students significant rights of access to their educational records. This act and the Buckley Amendment also protect the privacy of student records and require the institution to inform students of their rights and safeguards. For example, the institution cannot give a student's address and phone number to another individual who says he is the student's friend. Faculty and the institution cannot send grade reports to someone other than the individual student, not even to a parent or sponsor, without the student's written permission. Similarly, medical information or information from a counseling session cannot be disclosed to anyone without the student's permission. Modifications to these guidelines may be appropriate in times of national emergency or war. In addition, future U.S. legislation may alter what types of information government agencies can request. Faculty should stay abreast of regulations and use discretion in revealing confidential information to organizations or government officials.

Practices regarding what information is confidential and what information is not differ from country to country, so ESL students, parents, and sponsors are often confused by these U.S. laws and practices. For example, in some countries parents regularly receive their children's grades and can call the intsructors to ask how their children are performing. In contrast, in the United States, if parents or others wish to receive college students' grades and periodic reports, students must sign a standard letter or permission form supplied by the institution. Some policies and guidelines are uniform across U.S. postsecondary institutions whereas others differ slightly from institution to institution. Therefore, faculty should be familiar with their institutions' policies and guidelines regarding such issues as well as with the U.S. laws.

Some situations are more serious than reporting grades or giving information. In cases where the student is in danger, faculty need to take decisive action which may include contacting parents or relatives. Ultimately the most ethical action is for faculty to consider what's best for the student.

Beyond the instances that legally require confidentiality are other situations where confidentiality seems ethical and appropriate (e.g., highly personal stories, political views, financial information). Again, issues of confidentiality are often not clear-cut. Should other faculty know that student X is taking medication for depression or that student Y is having marital problems? Should faculty know that student Z has been stalking another ESL student, has been taken into custody by campus police several times, and told not to speak to the student? Above all, faculty have the responsibility to respect the privacy and the rights of students and treat them humanely while at the same time attending to the welfare of others, students and faculty, and abiding by U.S. laws and institutional guidelines.

These two closely connected factors—the power differential and issues of confidentiality—play an important role in faculty and student interactions. In this section, we examine these factors and ethical dimensions of several areas of interactions outside the classroom. In chapter 8, we look at faculty responsibilities regarding advising and personal relationships. ESL students may turn to faculty seeking advice on numerous aspects of living in the United States and may be confused by common U.S. faculty–student relationships and interactions outside of class. In chapter 9, we discuss faculty's role in seeing that students are as safe as possible while living in the United States and that they understand and practice safe behavior. Finally, in chapter 10, we examine the ethical and cultural dimensions of gift giving, a generally pleasant but at times confusing social practice, one that is again complicated by issues of power. Because of their power and authority, faculty can have a positive influence on students.

CHAPTER

8

Advising and Personal Relationships

Scenario One

Mrs. Garcia had taught ESL at the community college level for years. She felt that having students keep journals was an extremely good way for them to practice informal writing. She required them to write at least three times per week. She collected the journals once a week and generally responded to one entry for each student. At the beginning of the semester she had told the students that if anyone wrote something that she considered dangerous, she would have to report this to her program administrator. About the middle of the semester Katarina Tivetsky, a refugee, related in her journal that she was reading a book on ways the terminally ill could end their lives by their own hand. Mrs. Garcia was worried about Katarina. She appeared distracted, was often late to class, and seldom participated. She did not seem to have many friends. Mrs. Garcia wondered if Katarina were depressed, ill, or considering suicide.

Scenario Two

Ali Inal, a 20-year-old from Istanbul, Turkey, was excited to be studying in the United States. He had never lived away from his family before and was surprised by all the freedom he had. In contrast, his life in Turkey had been very structured and his responsibilities clear. Ali was an average student who occasionally missed class or failed to complete his homework. After Ali had been at the intensive English program for about a month, his father called Miss Rupert, an instructor whom Ali had mentioned to his father as being very helpful. Mr. Inal asked Miss Rupert to keep an eye on his son and inform him if he did not come to class or do his work. The father said that he would call every 2 weeks for a report on his son and asked that Miss Rupert call him if there were lapses in Ali's attendance or work. He then gave Miss Rupert his phone number and his fax number.

Scenario Three

Mrs. Wallingford asked Christiane Beaufort to baby sit for her 7-year-old daughter, Chloe. Christiane was a responsible student and had been in Mrs. Wallingford's class for two semesters. In addition, Christiane had met Chloe before, as Mrs. Wallingford had brought Chloe to several school functions and fieldtrips. Chloe liked Christiane and Christiane seemed to enjoy seeing Chloe. When asked to baby sit, Christiane was reluctant to refuse and, therefore, agreed. Christiane and Chloe had fun that evening and Mrs. Wallingford felt that Christiane had done an excellent job. When Mrs. Wallingford tried to pay her, Christiane said, "No, you don't need to pay," because she felt strange accepting payment from her teacher. In addition, she may have realized that with a student visa she was not legally allowed to work off campus.

Scenario Four

A popular young instructor, Ms. Schaffenhauser, took special care to get to know each of the students in her class and to build an open, respectful atmosphere in the classroom. She and her students developed a good rapport and sometimes did things together outside of class as a group. For example, she would often spend the break after her class chatting with students. One Friday night they all went to a movie and had pizza afterwards. Another time a student who had an apartment invited everyone in the class to her apartment for a potluck dinner. One of the men in the class, Hector Alvarado from Venezuela, invited Ms. Schaffenhauser to dinner at an expensive restaurant. She politely refused. A week or so later, he invited Ms. Schaffenhauser to a concert. Again, she politely refused, suggesting that he ask all the class to go to a movie or dance club. He replied that he would like to take her to the concert and did not want to go with the class. She thanked him for the invitation but again declined. For spring break this young man took a trip to Las Vegas. When he returned, he came to Ms. Schaffenhauser's office and presented her with a gold necklace, explaining that it would look beautiful on her as she was so lovely.

ADVISING RESPONSIBILITIES

ESL faculty often find themselves in a position to do more than just teach English. They become advisors on academic as well as nonacademic issues. Faculty job descriptions may require a certain number of office hours and faculty may even be assigned advisees. In addition, students often seek advice from faculty after class or at school functions. What are faculty's advising responsibilities? When ESL students arrive in English-speaking countries for the first time, whether as international students, immigrants, or refugees, the first few weeks and even months can be quite difficult, as they generally face a new culture and a new way of life. They may be homesick and disoriented, with very few friends to help them out. Consequently, students may turn to their ESL instructors for help and advice. It is easy and relatively nonthreatening for them to ask a teacher. In fact, many curriculum materials actually teach the very kinds of things students ask most about, namely, life skills, such as reading want ads, making a doctor's appointment, and talking to a child's teacher. Most of the time the instructor can be of help (e.g., explaining to a student how to start the process of obtaining a driver's license). But, there are times when the role of advisor can be more complex, and instructors should proceed with caution.

In their book, *Intercultural Advising in English-Language Programs*, Coffey and Grace (1997) argued that certain qualities and skills are important for advisors. Their advice is offered to staff who have the job title of advisor, but their comments are equally valid for faculty who find themselves in advising roles. Coffey and Grace (1997) asserted that advisors need to have knowledge about themselves, about different cultures, and about adjusting to a new environment. Similarly emphasizing the importance of cultural understanding, Burak and Hoffa (2001) in their book, *Crisis Management in a Cross-Cultural Situation*, argued that "advance planning and cross-cultural sensitivity make all the difference in dealing with crises" (p. xix). When defining important knowledge about self, Coffey and Grace (1997) listed the following characteristics:

> knowledge of the values, attitudes, and preferred communication styles in your culture; awareness of the stereotypical views one holds about members of various cultures; knowledge of the values, attitudes, and communication styles that you find offensive or irritating in other cultures; and knowledge of your position on the continuum of ethnorelativism. The goal is to recognize and appreciate cultural differences as viable alternatives. (pp. 3–4)

They also list eight personal qualities that make for effective advising: "(a) interest in and respect for cultural differences, (b) tolerance for ambiguous situations, (c) open-mindedness, (d) empathy, (e) flexibility and adaptability, (f) sense of humor, (g) warmth in human relationships, and (h) perceptiveness" (pp. 4–5). Coffey and Grace (1997) differentiated between these eight qualities and certain skills that help advisors be effective. These skills, which can be learned, include talking with nonnative speakers of English, being a good listener, drawing students out, using nonverbal communication effectively, knowing how to say "no," dealing with strong emotions, and knowing how to end a conversation (p. 6).

Unlike individuals who are assigned advising duties, faculty are often surprised to find themselves in the position of advisor. In fact, students may communicate their problems in a variety of ways. Many times, they seek advice at inopportune moments, just before class is scheduled to begin or during a short break. Many students are unfamiliar with office hours and their purpose. In orienting students to the U.S. academic community and accepted student behavior, faculty can explain office hours the first day of class and then follow up with another explanation about a week later. It is sometimes helpful to schedule appointments with students just to get them accustomed to the concept of faculty office hours and to allow them to see for themselves how faculty office hours work. Another way students may communicate to an instructor is through a journal entry. Many writing instructors, like Mrs. Garcia in Scenario One, now require journal writing as a part of their regular course assignments. Sometimes problems will be mentioned in the journal rather than face to face. In addition, ESL students may prefer to communicate by e-mail. In that way, they can avoid face-to-face interaction and can plan in advance just what they want to say. Many ESL students find it a very safe medium to communicate their issues and problems.

In advising situations, teachers must be aware of the power their words and actions may have and must respect students' confidentiality. Students must know that their journals will be held in strictest confidence. They should also be taught to realize that although an e-mail to a teacher may seem confidential, and the instructor will try to keep it so, it may not be. E-mails are more public than people often realize. For example, if a person is sent an e-mail, he or she can easily forward it to others. E-mails may also be monitored at work. Additionally, it is easy to send e-mails to the wrong individuals or to a group unintentionally. This is not to suggest, however, that the use of e-mail be discouraged. For simple, straightforward problems it is convenient, quick, and easy.

Although students must be assured of confidentiality, especially with journals, they must also be clearly told on the first day of class that some issues will trigger action on the part of the instructor (e.g., evidence of physical abuse or domestic violence, threats of violence, knowledge of illegal activities). This is probably what Mrs. Garcia was thinking about in Scenario

One when she read Katarina's journal entry about a book on suicide. Students need to realize that if they write about or describe a potentially dangerous situation, teachers will inform those within academic institutions who can help. On the other hand, Katarina seemed not to recall this information, possibly because she was calling for help. Mrs. Garcia should first talk to Katarina to offer a sympathetic ear and suggest she go to the counseling center. As a precaution, Ms. Garcia should also alert the director of the program. Ms. Garcia needs to continue to monitor the situation as a single discussion or referral may not solve the problem. She also needs to be mindful of respecting Katarina's privacy and the confidentiality of her personal information.

Knowing what is confidential information and what is not may be confusing for faculty. Coffey and Grace (1997) suggested that programs have "a written policy explicitly stating the program's confidentiality rules" and ". . . consider writing a policy information sheet" for faculty and staff (p. 20). If a language program is part of a larger institution that has a confidentiality statement, that statement applies to the language program. Thus, it should be circulated among faculty and staff.

An important part of a confidentiality statement is the subject of making referrals. Instructors need to recognize the limits of their expertise and need to know when and how to make referrals. "One of the most valuable skills for an in-house intercultural adviser [faculty member] is knowing when and how to refer a student to other needed professional support services" (Coffey & Grace, 1997, p. 97). It is tempting to try to help students solve their problems, but serious problems require professional help.

According to Coffey and Grace, "Trying to handle the situation alone, . . . is unprofessional and unethical and may actually prolong or worsen the student's difficulties" (p. 100).

Although this is sound advice, it is often hard for instructors to determine when they can handle a problem themselves with some sympathy and advice, and when they need to refer students to professional counseling. Bishop (1997) stated that this difficulty may become particularly evident in writing classes, where students are much more likely to reveal personal problems in essays and journals. She explores the role of the writing teacher as therapist, and although she agrees that writing teachers should refer students with problems to counselors, she feels that that advice is not always adequate. She lists ambiguous and problematic situations in which she has found herself, situations in which the standard "send them to the counseling center" advice was not enough. She encourages instructors, and program administrators, to educate themselves about students' psychological issues, and about resources available on and off campus. For example, counseling centers at postsecondary institutions periodically conduct workshops for faculty and staff on how to recognize students who are under considerable stress and how to deal with unruly behavior. Workshops on these topics and such information can be invaluable for faculty as well as staff. Further, Bishop encourages teacher education programs to include the topic of counseling, and encourages composition scholars and teachers to share their experiences in their conferences and publications.

Teachers' referrals to counseling centers are most commonly made because of psychological, medical, and substance abuse issues. Psychological problems are viewed differently in different cultures, with many cultures viewing any type of counseling as negative. Burak and Hoffa (2001) pointed out that international students may not be comfortable talking to a perceived stranger and that the U.S. concept of *counseling* is often unfamiliar to individuals from other cultures. Early in the semester, faculty can inform all students of the availability of counseling services and help students realize that in the United States, seeking help at a counseling center or through a support group is considered acceptable. Students need to realize that these services are not just for the mentally ill, but for students of all types with a variety of problems. Perhaps the most important psychological difficulty for an instructor to monitor is threatened suicide, as was, possibly, the case with Katarina in Scenario One. Although this is not a common occurrence, it does happen, and most suicide victims hint about what they are considering. Even a seemingly insignificant spoken or written comment such as "You would be better off without me," or "You wouldn't like me if you really knew me," can be clues and must be taken seriously. Certainly instructors are well within their rights and responsibilities to call such a student aside and ask for further clarification of these kinds of statements. If a student reports feeling low or a little blue, a teacher should urge going for help immediately. If student A reports concerns about student B, it is again a good idea to approach student B with a general opener such as, "Some of the other students are a little worried about you. Are you feeling well? How are you getting along here?" On occasion it may be wise, with the student's permission, to make the appointment and then actually accompany the student to the appropriate office. In any case it is important to take action and to alert the program administrator.

In addition to psychological problems, ESL teachers need to be alert to signs of medical and substance abuse. If something is clearly wrong, such as a severe persistent cough, or the inability to stay awake in class, it is important to approach the student. This can be difficult. Sometimes a leading question can open up the subject. "Are you feeling well? You've looked a little tired lately." It is now up to the student to decide whether or not to pursue the line of conversation. At this point it may be wise to refer the student to the appropriate medical facilities, although she or he cannot be forced to go. Sometimes, poorer students may, in fact, be quite ill, but unable to afford medical care and too proud to mention it. Instructors may wish to help students understand their options regarding available services. There may be free clinics or other public services at the institution or in the area. In addition, if a student requires time off or needs to turn in an assignment late, it is probably wise to make that accommodation. Sometimes, the idea that an instructor could legitimately excuse an absence is a new idea to students from other cultures.

Yet where does a faculty member draw the line if a student has ongoing psychological or medical problems? Students may not follow through on a referral or may not follow the advice or treatment recommended by a counselor or medical doctor. Treating all students fairly may mean that a student with a substance abuse problem fails classes. Faculty cannot allow a student with a substance abuse problem, for example, to be excused from attending class regularly or completing assignments, if she or he is not getting counseling and treatment. Whether or not the student is in treatment, if the student is not able to fulfill the requirements of the class, the faculty member can help her or him by explaining options. These may include helping the student to drop the class, take a leave of absence, or withdraw from the institution.

A related problem is that of the disruptive student. Faculty need to be clear about the consequences for poor performance or disruptive behavior and, within reason, need to hold all students to the same standards. Disruptive behavior threatens others and cannot be tolerated. (See chap. 3 for discussion of unruly behavior.) As with the students with psychological or substance abuse problems, faculty need to make clear their expectations, and the consequences of negative behavior or not doing the assigned work for the class. Again, students who do not seek treatment, or improve on their own, may receive failing grades and may be advised to withdraw from the class or from the institution. Throughout, faculty need to balance the needs of the disruptive student with those of the other students, the teacher, the program, and the institution.

Not all advising situations present a crisis or call for immediate action. Occasionally students ask for advice on problematic matters or simply confide in faculty. For example, if a female student from a culture where women are still considered oppressed by Western standards complains that her husband constantly belittles her, what should an instructor do? One might be tempted to suggest that she consider marriage counseling, standing up for her rights or divorce, but such advice would probably not take into account the student's cultural, social, and financial background. It might be best simply to serve as a thoughtful listener and make her aware of available resources such as hotlines, support groups, relevant publications, and women's organizations.

When appropriate, faculty need to tell students of their legal rights and options. A student may confide in her instructor that she has had several items stolen from her dormitory room, is receiving obscene phone calls late at night, or is being harassed by an ex-boyfriend, or that her friend was raped at a party over the weekend. In each case, there are steps the student can take, but she may not be aware of them. In the case of stolen items, the faculty member can remind the student to always lock the door when leaving, and suggest reporting the theft to her Resident Advisor (RA) in the dormitory. The RA may then contact the campus police if the student wishes to file a report. In the case of obscene phone calls, the type of action the student can take depends on where she lives. On campus, the RA can be told. Then, the student's phone number can be changed and the new number unlisted. Off campus, the student can contact the phone company and have her number changed to an unlisted one and, depending upon the type and frequency of the phone calls, may wish to contact the city police. Regardless of what the faculty member thinks should be done in these examples, the individual student must make the decision to file a complaint or not. Even if a faculty member feels certain that a student was harassed or raped, she cannot officially report it. She can, however, give the student information about support groups and counseling for victims of such crimes. In all these examples, faculty need to tell students their rights and assist them if they can. An offer to call the campus police or accompany the student to file a complaint with the appropriate office often makes the process less intimidating for the student.

ESL instructors must be ever vigilant with regard to the health and well being of their students and realize that requests for advice can come in many forms. Faculty must also be ever mindful of moral and legal issues of confidentiality and alert students to their rights. Maintaining confidentiality even applies to parents and guardians wishing information about their children, as mandated by the Family Educational Rights and Privacy Act and the Buckley Amendment. By U.S. law, Mr. Inal, in Scenario Two, cannot check up on his son's progress without his son's permission. Miss Rupert, Ali's teacher, needs to convey this regulation to Ali's father and to Ali, even at the risk that Ali will be angry with his father for attempting to check up on him. Institutions may have waiver forms that students can sign to allow parents or others to have access to such information. An English language program may also wish to draft such a letter to have available for students who wish to keep their parents or others informed of their progress.

Although faculty need to be mindful of issues of confidentiality, in cases of danger, there are times intervention is necessary. This intervention may mean contacting parents or other relatives. If, for example, it becomes evident that a young student has a serious eating disorder, faculty or an administrator need to intervene (e.g., referrals to counseling and medical professionals). If attempts at intervention are not successful, and the student seems to be staying the same or getting worse, then a faculty member or administrator has an ethical obligation to inform the parents as quickly as possible.

Helping students who have serious psychological and health problems is stressful. Faculty have busy schedules with numerous obligations, and advising may not be an assigned duty with additional compensation. Advising nonnative speakers may be particularly time consuming as there are language barriers as well as cultural barriers. Students may count on their teachers for support, because they are far from their usual support systems and may need extra help in adjusting to their situations. Often they do not know where else to turn for help. Advising can take an emotional, physical, and spiritual toll on faculty and can "affect both job performance and emotional well-being" (Coffey & Grace, 1997, p. 64). Faculty need to take care of themselves physically and emotionally, develop a support system among colleagues, know their own limitations and time constraints, keep up with current issues, not demand perfection from themselves, and learn how to say "no" (Coffey & Grace, 1997; Monroe, 1991). Faculty should not hesitate to contact professionals for advice on how to handle a particular situation, especially a serious one. In sum, faculty need to realize that they do not have to "take care" of situations all by themselves.

RESPONSIBILITIES AND PERSONAL RELATIONSHIPS

Faculty have the responsibility to treat students humanely, with respect, and without showing favoritism, both inside and outside the classroom. The power differential between faculty and students can be problematic in situations where personal relationships or arrangements are made. In Scenario Three, for example, a request to baby sit may seem harmless. On one level, Christiane may enjoy spending time with Mrs. Wallingford's daughter, Chloe, but she may have felt obligated to baby sit when asked by her teacher. The situation was then even further complicated when Christiane would have been technically breaking INS regulations by accepting pay for work done off campus. Granted, one evening babysitting does not constitute having a job off campus, but Mrs. Wallingford should strictly follow INS regulations and should not put Christiane in the awkward position of either possibly offending her teacher or breaking INS laws. This scenario highlights the fact that even asking students for small favors can have unforeseen complications.

ESL faculty must take care to avoid exploiting students through coercion (even if unintentional), threats, or sexual harassment. Exploitation could be something as seemingly innocent as an instructor asking students for help in learning their language. This type of behavior is generally harmless but can be abused if, for example, an instructor coerces a student into spending much time, in essence, "tutoring" him or her. Because of the power vested in the faculty member, the student may feel unable to refuse to help the instructor. Certainly it is inappropriate for the instructor to attempt to practice the language during class, as it robs the student of time to practice English, the target language.

Students may also be exploited when they are used as sources of other types of information (e.g., information about their countries or political information). Issues of confidentiality may also apply in such situations. A faculty member working on an article or book about a particular issue or country should avoid using students as sources of information unless the students agree to do so and are given appropriate credit. Similarly, students should not regularly be asked to serve as translators without compensation. One ESL instructor relates the time when a group of activists attempting to locate missing servicemen in Vietnam approached her about using class time to assist in their project. They wanted to ask students questions and have them try to identify pictures of U.S. servicemen. Clearly it would have been inappropriate for the instructor to grant this request.

Tutoring and financial arrangements between instructors and students can also lead to situations of exploitation. Because learning a new language is a daunting task, students may opt for private tutoring in conjunction with their formal classroom studies. Sometimes they approach their instructors requesting tutoring. A program or institution may have regulations forbidding an instructor from tutoring his or her own students. But even if this activity is not banned, it seems ill-advised, as tutoring one's own students can be seen as a conflict of interest and appears to show favoritism. Ideally, issues of tutoring one's own students would be discussed among all members of the program and a program-wide policy developed. A program might, for example, develop a policy stating that instructors may not tutor students who are currently in their classes, and develop a list of possible tutors who do not teach in the program. The tutors could be M.A. TESL or certificate students or others who are qualified. The cost of tutoring sessions could be set by the program, and the program could refer students to the tutors or to appropriate campus facilities such as writing and learning centers. Along with the ethical issue of tutoring is a cultural dimension. Many students, some Asians in particular, are accustomed to paying for additional tutoring in cram schools. Although such businesses are emerging in the United States (e.g., Princeton Review, TOEFL preparation courses, Kumon Math), this system is not as readily followed in the United States as in some other countries. Therefore, requesting tutoring may seem quite natural to some ESL students, and instructors may receive several requests. Having policies in place regarding tutoring is wise.

Social relationships are yet another area where faculty need to exercise caution. Social interactions among faculty and students outside of class can enhance students' language and cultural experiences and can be enjoyable for all involved. At the same time, faculty should consider how their actions may be interpreted. Students' cultural expectations may complicate faculty-student relationships, as may be the case in Scenario Four, where Hector Alvarado is obviously attracted to Ms. Schaffenhauser. ESL students are often surprised by the informality and friendliness of faculty members in and out of the classroom. They may be unaccustomed to instructors dressing informally, asking students to address them by their first name, having coffee with students after class or going on outings with students. Students may interpret friendliness as an invitation for a social relationship, or even as coercion. They may feel it is necessary to comply with a faculty member's wishes in order to get a good grade or even pass the course. In addition, gestures of friendship and concern from an instructor may be seen as unwanted advances by a student. Faculty must take care not to show favoritism, to suggest romantic or sexual interest in a student, or to exert pressure on a student to comply with certain requests. Certainly there are instances of a student and professor having fallen in love while the student is taking the professor's class. However, romantic relationships should be delayed until after the student has finished the program. Faculty contracts and institutional policies often specifically forbid such relationships with students, with faculty job termination as the possible final consequence.

Ms. Schaffenhauser, in Scenario Four, should not accept the necklace, and should explain to Hector the policies of her institution. (Also see chap. 10 on gift giving.) She may wish to inform her supervisor of the situation. If, at this point, Hector, drops the issue, the problem is resolved. However, if he continues to pursue his teacher, she can ask her supervisor to move Hector to another class and to speak to Hector, telling him that his actions are inappropriate and that disciplinary action will be taken if he persists in pursuing her. In an extreme case, if Hector continues to pursue Ms. Schaffenhauser, it may be considered sexual harassment, or stalking. In such a case, Ms. Schaffenhauser should take the necessary steps to stop Hector's actions. This may include speaking to the police and filing charges against Hector.

The majority of interactions among faculty and students are positive, and provide both faculty and students much satisfaction. Yet issues surrounding interactions among faculty and students outside of the classroom are complex. With ESL students, faculty advising and faculty–student relationships are further complicated by language difficulties and by differences in cultural practices, attitudes, and understandings. Faculty have the responsibility to attend to the whole person and to treat each student fairly and with respect and humanity. They need to keep in mind the power differential between themselves and students, the limitations of their own abilities, the confidentiality of sensitive information, the legal rights of students, and their own well being. Faculty and student interactions are important for students in learning the language, in acculturating to U.S. culture and academe, and in growing intellectually and personally. These interactions often are determining factors in students being successful and having positive experiences in the United States. They also provide faculty job satisfaction and psychological rewards.

CHAPTER

9

Student Safety

Scenario One

On being asked in his community college ESL class what he had done over the weekend, Farid Homayouni told his classmates and teacher that he and his friends had been out late at a disco and gotten into a fight. Farid was a 22-year-old student from Iran whose family had recently moved to a large city in the United States. Farid enjoyed having a good time, frequently going to clubs, restaurants, and discos. He had a lot of friends and dated many young women. He openly talked about the situation that past weekend, and the teacher, Mr. Simpson, soon realized that Farid had gone alone to one of the less safe neighborhoods in his city. Mr. Simpson spoke, in a nonjudgmental way, about the possible dangers of such neighborhoods and situations. He, Farid, and the other students then brainstormed suggestions about how to avoid such situations, and how to deal with situations once one is already involved.

Scenario Two

Emily Monti, a teenaged student from France who was attending a small private college, enjoyed going shopping at the big department stores located in the downtown area of the large city where she lived. Unfortunately, even in the elegant and expensive areas where such stores were located, and particularly in the surrounding areas just a block or two away, there were a number of people panhandling (asking passing strangers on the street for money). On one occasion, a panhandler reached out toward Emily in a way that she found threatening, and she became frightened and ran away. For many weeks after this incident, Emily didn't venture far away from her home or school.

Scenario Three

Mrs. Sandra Gomes, a middle-aged immigrant from Central America, lived in an area of her city that was quite far from the adult school she was attending at night. Although she worked full time during the day, as did her husband, her family did not have much money. They did not have a car, so she took the bus to her night class, and her clothes were simple and worn. Although she did not complain, she did express some worries about traveling on the bus alone at night, and walking from the bus stop to her home at the end of the evening. Her teacher, Mr. Javier Orozco, was impressed by Mrs. Gomes' dedication to her classes, and her hard work, but he was also concerned about her safety. He did not know what to do about her situation, beyond giving general advice about being careful.

SAFETY ISSUES

International and immigrant students, especially younger students, have concerns about their safety, as do their families. Those who work with them have concerns about the safety of their students, but may wonder what their role can or should be in educating them about safety and in helping them stay safe in the United States. In the not-too-distant past (until the late 1960s), U.S. colleges and universities saw themselves as *in loco parentis* to students, both domestic and international, and thus were able, for example, to impose rules about curfews and to maintain separate dormitories for females and males. This parental view of the institution's role has changed, particularly with the increasing number of adult students on campuses throughout the United States. Now college students are assumed to be independent adults who are basically responsible for their own behavior. Curfews, separate dormitories, strict visiting hours, and other restrictions are artifacts of the past at most universities today. And the issue of dormitories does not even apply in the cases of most adult schools and community colleges.

Placing fewer restrictions on students and more of the responsibility for their own actions in students' hands does not mean institutions have no obligation to ensure students' safety. In fact, universities and colleges have liabilities and legal responsibilities regarding the safety of students enrolled in their programs in the United States and abroad (e.g., Kast, 1997/1998). An Interorganizational Task Force on Health and Safety in Study Abroad, with

NAFSA: Association of International Educators as a member, developed a set of "guidelines designed to promote health and safety in study abroad," including evaluating health and safety aspects of each program, and providing students and parents with information and orientation regarding health and safety issues (Safety, p. 54).

In addition to institutional obligations to provide safe environments for students, ESL faculty have an even more important ethical obligation to help students be safe inside and outside the classroom, and are in an ideal position to do so. ESL teachers have a responsibility to their students to educate them about safety issues, whatever their age or situation, especially if they are new to the United States or to a certain city or area. And those teachers are in fact uniquely positioned to provide this kind of education and advice (without, of course, being intrusive or overly directive). Faculty are in a position of authority and have the power to influence students' actions. This means that faculty need to balance their advice regarding safety issues so that students practice safe behaviors and reduce their risks of harm, yet at the same time are not so fearful that they do not venture out and enjoy living and studying in the United States.

To understand how to deal with safety issues, two factors related to safety seem important. First, the concept of safe behavior is not simple or monolithic; it is culturally and socially constructed. What constitutes safe behavior in a student's home country may be dangerous behavior in the United States. For example, it may be common to carry large amounts of cash in a student's home country, but this practice is unwise in the United States. Another example of cultural differences in this regard might be judgments of how women dress and behave in public; interpretations of the safety of certain clothing or behavior may vary widely. Second, international and immigrant students and their families, especially those new to the United States, often have an unrealistic view of how safe or how dangerous life in the United States is. The United States may be perceived as having become more dangerous recently, even though the crime rate has actually declined in recent years. And a student who has a bad experience, or a threatening experience, as Emily did in Scenario Two, is likely to become afraid to go out at all.

Often students arrive in the United States with a peculiar mixture of fear and naiveté. They experience fear because they have seen American movies and television shows, and read and seen coverage of national and local news events. These often give the somewhat exaggerated impression that the United States is a violent, crime-filled country. On the other hand, these students are naïve about the reality of certain dangers, as Farid seemed to be in Scenario One, in which he was out late in an area generally considered unsafe. Farid seemed to have made little effort to find out about the part of town where the club was situated. Students may be naïve about dangers that may exist in different places and from different sources than they imagine. For example, they may worry about being mugged on the street at night, but they may not be wary enough of the motives of a con man, or of a perpetrator of acquaintance rape. This naiveté may be compounded in some cases by the fact that some immigrants and international students come from privileged backgrounds, and may have been somewhat shielded from danger and unpleasantness in their countries. On the other hand, some students may be quite poor, and their very poverty can expose them to more dangerous situations, such as living in high-crime areas. Mrs. Gomes, in Scenario Three, had to ride the bus, and walk, alone at night because she could not afford a car. These actions put her at more risk than if she drove or lived in a safe neighborhood.

Although their concerns may be exaggerated, or perhaps misdirected, students and their families are right to be concerned. Crime is an ever-present danger. Even the safest campuses and cities have crime. Students have been injured and killed in the United States. Because of this reality, our ethical obligation to help students stay safe is clear.

A related ethical issue is that of race and crime. Some ESL students have been victims of crime, at least in part because of their racial or ethnic background. This is a difficult topic to address, but teachers may need to do so. Another aspect of this issue of race and crime is that many students who come here from elsewhere bring stereotypes about which racial groups commit crimes in the United States. Some students then react with fear and other negative feelings toward members of certain racial groups, notably African Americans. Teachers can talk about the unfairness of stereotyping in a variety of contexts, including but not limited to the issue of crime, and try to lead students away from unjust generalizations. Most students do not want to be racist, but have been inculcated with preconceptions about racial groups, preconceptions that are perhaps fostered by media portrayals. Addressing these preconceptions is an opportunity to promote better understanding and more social justice for all racial and ethnic groups.

STUDENT CONCERNS

For instructors wondering how to carry out their ethical obligation to help students stay safe, information about students' views and knowledge can be very helpful. The results of a survey of 58 international students at the University of San Francisco (Hafernik, Vandrick, & Messerschmitt, 2000) may be helpful in this regard. In this study, several themes emerged. First, the international students surveyed were interested in learning more about how to be safe while in the United States, and wanted their campus to take a proactive stance on safety. Both male and female respondents felt that a wide range of safety issues was important, issues such as knowing how to avoid being robbed or attacked, knowing how to be safe in the home, knowing how to prevent sexual assault, and knowing what to do in an emergency.

Second, international students may not be aware of what services are available on campus. Universities often provide such services as an escort service on campus and within a limited area near campus, free self-defense classes, showings of safety videos and group discussions, guest speakers, safety brochures and literature, safety programs in the dormitories, articles with safety tips in the campus newspaper, and support groups for individuals who have been victims of crimes. Many students, however, do not know about these services. Also students may not be aware that they should call the campus police in certain situations (e.g., a purse or books are stolen, a suspicious person is on campus). Therefore, by informing students of what the campus police and others on campus can do, we may be able to improve their safety.

Finally, a third theme emerging from the data in the survey is that students may unknowingly put themselves into risky situations, may not be able to judge what a dangerous situation is, and may not know how to get out of uncomfortable situations. This may be especially true for females. Although from different positions and for different reasons, both Emily in Scenario Two, and Mrs. Gomes in Scenario Three, felt fearful about being out late at night. Both Emily and Mrs. Gomes, like students who responded to the survey, were unsure how to handle precarious situations. They spoke of being out late at night in an area where they did not feel safe. Student responses to the survey suggest that any discussion of safety issues should include the following: how to deal with strangers asking for money; how to get rid of people who follow one; when and where it is safe to go alone; and how to call a cab.

PEDAGOGICAL STRATEGIES

ESL programs and faculty may find it useful to hold faculty meetings devoted to safety issues, talk to students about their safety concerns, and devise ways to systematically incorporate the discussion of safety issues into programs. The following specific suggestions may be helpful (Hafernik, Vandrick, & Messerschmitt, 1999). From time to time, teachers or administrators can undertake surveys of ESL students regarding safety, such as the one described earlier. Actual student data can be very useful in designing and implementing the content of safety programs and orientations. In addition, the general topic of safety and safe behaviors should be part of an institution's orientation for new students. As well as providing information, the orientation could include campus police officers giving a short presentation. This serves two functions: showing international students that U.S. police officers can be friendly, approachable, and helpful; and reminding campus police officers that there is an international student population on campus.

ESL faculty can also distribute and go over campus safety brochures and student handbooks, agreeing upon a specific class in which this will be done. Material can be given out at the orientation but follow-up activities in a particular class are advisable. This could be as simple as a scanning exercise in reading class to locate specific information such as the campus police phone number, the services provided by the campus escort service, and the phone number for public transportation information. Faculty can also agree upon specific safety issues to be covered in particular classes. For example, the oral communication class could cover personal safety on campus (e.g., not leaving belongings unattended, consistently locking dorm rooms, reporting suspicious individuals to the campus police). This could be done through numerous activities such as watching videos, doing role playing, and presenting public announcement bulletins. A class focusing on reading and writing skills could cover safety issues related to health (e.g., AIDS, alcohol and drugs, sexual assault); a computer class could find and evaluate websites related to health and safety.

Program personnel can post safety-related information such as the following: safety workshops, first-aid information, services provided by campus police, and numbers to call in an emergency. Announcements of workshops and events can also be made in class. The campus or local newspaper is another source of materials and information for classes. For example, the campus newspaper may have a feature article on drinking on college campuses or date rape and the local television station may have news clips about car safety or hate crimes.

Students' own comments and stories, in and out of class, also provide the basis of lessons, perhaps mini "safety lessons." If students mention, as Farid, Emily, and Sandra all did in the three scenarios earlier, that they have been in unsafe situations, the teacher may want to use this as an opportunity to discuss safety issues. These lessons can be tailored to deal with safety issues particular to one's geographical area. For example, in urban areas there are often homeless people who panhandle, but students may not know how to handle such situations. In more rural areas, it may be that students should avoid dark, deserted areas late at night. Finally, faculty should make students aware of and draw on campus and local services such as the counseling center, health clinic, and student clubs including international clubs. These offices and groups usually have brochures outlining their services, offer free workshops, and provide speakers to classes.

Although the foregoing discussion has focused on safety issues related to preventing crime, ESL programs may also wish to work with students to prepare for natural and other disasters such as fire, earthquakes, floods, tornadoes, hurricanes, and terrorism. The principles in teaching about such natural disasters and terrorist attacks are much the same as in teaching about crime: Teachers need to provide their students with correct and useful information in accessible ways, while not frightening them.

Regarding teaching student safety issues, the following guidelines may be useful. First, ESL instructors can (and should) help students be informed, alert, and, therefore, safer in the United States. Second, helping students feel and be safe is an ongoing process. Teachers need to be ever vigilant and seize opportunities to address these issues. Third, teachers shouldn't worry about giving seemingly obvious advice (although of course such advice should never be given in a condescending way or in a way that ignores students' own knowledge); students often lack basic information about safety in the United States. Fourth, basic safety issues should be covered systematically, not left to chance: that is, programs can divide up the issues among various classes and workshops, in order that all important issues are covered. Finally, ESL programs and instructors need to present a balanced picture so that students are safety conscious but not afraid to go out and explore their cities and surroundings. Education is the key. Although ESL teachers cannot prevent all problems or protect their students at all times, they should do all they can to educate international students in ways that will help them avoid traumatic events. Doing so is an ethical obligation and a way of promoting social justice.

CHAPTER

10

Gift Giving

Scenario One

Dahmane and Malek Derdouri, brothers from Algeria, were taking classes in a university ESL program. Although they were pleasant people, they were not attending class regularly and were not doing well academically. About two thirds of the way through the semester, their parents invited two of their teachers, Susan Mott and Lorna Shillett, to dinner at a restaurant serving Algerian food. When the teachers arrived at the elegant restaurant, they found several members of the students' extended family awaiting them, along with a sumptuous feast. Course after course of beautifully presented and delicious food arrived, accompanied by several bottles of expensive wine. Everyone was gracious, and the evening was lovely. Later, as the teachers looked ahead to the time when they would have to give the two students grades, they felt a nagging sense of unease.

Scenario Two

Ms. Hamadian, an administrator in an ESL program at a private school with higher-than-average tuition, received a telephone call from an administrator at another university in another part of the state, asking her if she could help a young woman immigrant from Indonesia whom he knew, who wanted to study English. Ms. Hamadian agreed to meet the student, Rose Budra, and set up an appointment with her. When Rose came into the office, she appeared somewhat frantic. After introducing herself and making some small talk, Rose presented Ms. Hamadian with a colorful, inexpensive scarf, "as a sign of respect." Rose then told the director of her great desire to attend English classes at Ms. Hamadian's institution, but stated that she had almost no money, sometimes not even enough to buy food. She begged the director to allow her to attend classes without paying tuition.

Scenario Three

Students in Professor Ana Santoso's advanced ESL writing class were assigned a 10-page research paper. One student from Hong Kong, Jun Tsai, had a particularly difficult time choosing a topic, finding appropriate sources to read and discuss, and writing the paper. Professor Santoso spent many hours working with Mr. Tsai on this research project, which he had to revise several times. About a week before the paper was due, Professor Santoso found in her faculty mailbox a small, beautifully wrapped gift box containing a lovely, delicate, and clearly expensive silver bracelet. The accompanying card stated that the bracelet was a "small gift of thanks" for the professor's help with the student's research paper.

ESL professionals are sometimes given gifts by students, and often wonder when it is ethical and appropriate to accept gifts and when it is not. The issue is, as are some of the other issues we cover in this book, complicated by language and cultural issues as well as issues of power. Here we examine some of the gift-giving traditions found in the United States, especially those relevant to the classroom context, and how they may differ from the traditions of non-native students. Although gift giving practices are by no means monolithic throughout the United States, there are some that can be identified. Within the ESL context, gift giving can sometimes raise troubling ethical questions. We acknowledge that these situations are often ambiguous, and that it is perhaps impossible to completely separate cultural aspects and ethical aspects.

Normally, students' giving gifts to teachers is a gracious expression of thanks, creating a friendly feeling, particularly at the end of the course. Instructors in the United States who do not teach ESL often receive presents as well, especially at the holiday season or the end of the year, from grateful students. This cultural practice is particularly prevalent at the elementary level, and commercial greeting card companies even sell "teacher" cards appropriate for the occasion. It is generally considered quite a harmless tradition. In fact, such giving of presents is part of a long tradition of gift giving in European-American society, including gifts for birthdays, graduations, weddings and engagements, and as thanks for hospitality or assistance.

The giving of presents can be viewed as a scripted event in any culture. Hatch (1992) defined a script as "knowledge that people have of the structure of stereotypic event sequences" (p. 85). She pointed out that "when we move to another country or are functioning in another language, we may find that our scripts need to be radically amended" (p. 89). For example, in certain cultures, the gift giver must offer the gift with a certain hand or body motion, and the receiver must accept the gift with certain body motions (Morrison, Conaway, & Borden, 1994). The body language is, of course, in addition to the appropriate verbal language. These are examples of cultural differences; although they are important to know and follow, out of respect to other cultures, they do not seem to involve ethical issues or decisions.

ETHICAL ISSUES

Whereas many gift-giving scripts present only cultural dilemmas, others present ethical ones. Teachers sometimes feel uneasy about accepting presents and feel on some level that they have to make decisions that involve ethics. In some cases, they may wonder if something is, consciously or unconsciously, expected in return. Do international or immigrant students in the United States expect a present in return if they give teachers one? Do they ever expect a better grade in return for a gift? When does a gift become a bribe? On the other hand, do students feel they must give a present to their teachers even if doing so is a financial burden for them? When does a question of courtesy and custom become a question of ethics and, because of economic and power inequities, a question of social justice?

The issue of power may enter here. Gift giving may reflect the students' knowledge that teachers have authority and thus power over them. Students may feel obligated or compelled to give teachers gifts as an acknowledgment of that power, or to appease the teacher and therefore mitigate the consequences of that power. Students may feel even more obligated to give teachers gifts if they believe that such gift giving is customary, or if they see that other students do so. They may fear that if they do not follow suit, they will be considered wanting by the teacher, and thus may suffer negative consequences.

There are various factors that influence the appropriateness or inappropriateness of gift giving to teachers. The nature of the gift itself is important; some gifts seem to be acceptable, whereas others are not. Where do teachers draw the line between the acceptable and the unacceptable? Even if they find a particular present unacceptable, they may feel uncomfortable about refusing it, knowing that the refusal might be a serious breach of etiquette and hurt the student givers' feelings as well.

Items such as a pen and pencil set, a box of chocolates, a framed photograph, a gift certificate, or an invitation to dinner generally seem to be appropriate. A large cash gift would clearly be inappropriate. What are the defining features for appropriate and inappropriate gifts? Cash is probably inappropriate; gift certificates seem less so (but is this logical?). Inexpensive gifts, such as the scarf in Scenario Two, are probably acceptable, and refusing such gifts may be insulting. Gifts that are overly expensive, such as gold or other precious jewelry, are inappropriate; the silver bracelet offered to the writing instructor in Scenario Three is an example. Gifts that are overly personal are also inappropriate; for example, the gift of a silk nightgown would be both embarrassing and inappropriate, especially if given by a member of the opposite sex. These gifts need to be refused or returned, as tactfully as possible.

The timing of gift giving is also critical in determining whether or not it is an ethically acceptable gift. Timing can make the difference between a gift and a bribe, or at least the appearance of a bribe. Gifts given before an exam or when a student asks for a favor seem inappropriate. For example, a student's bringing a gift when asking to miss 2 weeks of class so she can go to the Grand Canyon, or when asking to turn in a paper late as she has an important exam in another class to study for, may be viewed as manipulative. Or giving an expensive gift before a major examination or other academic hurdle, as with the silver bracelet in Scenario Three, has too much of the appearance of a proffered bribe. Although Mr. Tsai may not in fact have intended the gift as a bribe, Professor Santoso should return this gift, both because of its value and because of its suspicious timing.

Unfortunately, many cases are more ambiguous than these. Scenario One, for example, involves a dinner, which is generally seen as more acceptable than an actual gift. However, because the dinner was so lavish and expensive, and because it was given toward the time when grades would be assigned, it could be interpreted as Dahmane's and Malek's, and their family members', trying, though indirectly, to influence Ms. Mott and Ms. Shillett, who would be giving those grades. The matter is complicated by the fact that the teachers did not realize until they reached the restaurant that the dinner would be so elaborate and expensive. Teachers need to use their best judgment in ambiguous cases such as this one, but in the actual event described here, it would have been far too rude and offensive for the teachers to leave the restaurant, insinuating that the hosts were trying to bribe the teachers.

The role of the gift giver herself or himself is also crucial. (Here we focus on students as the givers of gifts; however, parents, relatives, and adult friends of students may also give gifts.) Teachers often have special status in certain students' native cultures and, thus, giving the teacher a gift is an obligation in those cultures. According to Seward (1972), the Japanese, for example, feel a special sense of obligation to teachers and must try to repay these obligations. Some of the questions that arise are as follows: Is it appropriate to give the gift to an instructor in front of other students and faculty? Is a group gift more acceptable than an individual gift? How should the instructor respond: Open the gift in the presence of the giver, or wait until later to open it? In awkward gift-giving situations, what should an instructor or administrator do? In general, unless the gift is clearly unacceptable ethically, these questions are matters of respect and etiquette, and can generally be ascertained by learning about the students' cultural traditions in these areas.

If there is any doubt ethically, the recipient certainly needs to make it clear to the giver, politely and diplomatically of course, that the gift will not affect grades or special favors or exceptions to school policies. For example, a student gives a female administrator a batik shirt as the student is preparing to leave for 3 weeks mid-semester for her sister's wedding. She explains her situation and states her wish that she will still get good grades in her classes. Should the administrator refuse the gift? To refuse the gift may be viewed as an insult and may be at total variance with the student's cultural norms. What, however, is the administrator implying by accepting the gift?

In this case, as in most, there is not one correct answer. A possible course of action would be for the administrator to make sure the student has spoken individually to all her instructors and found out what work she will be missing; urge the student to do all the work she will miss by the time she returns; explain explicitly that her grades are determined by the teachers and that the administrator cannot influence her grades; and graciously accept the gift, knowing that it is not an expensive item. In the case of the scarf given in Scenario Two, the expectations of the gift giver are also relevant. But again, if the gift is inexpensive, and it is tactfully and clearly indicated to the student that the gift cannot and will not affect administrative decisions, then accepting the gift is probably the gracious course of action.

What seems most important in this situation and in others is that there be no suggestion of bribery, and that students clearly understand that gifts cannot buy grades or favors. To make the distinction between a gift and a bribe clear to students, it may be better to refuse a gift given before an exam and to explain tactfully, without any negative implications about the student or the current situation, why one cannot accept any gifts in this situation.

One possible way to minimize confusion and difficulties arising from differing gift-giving practices and expectations is to forbid all gifts on a program-wide basis. However, programs that have tried this have found it ineffective (P. Larson, personal communication, January 4, 1995). Students still find ways to give gifts. Programs and classes can, however, include instruction on gift-giving practices in the curriculum, being sure to include discussion of the elements discussed before (the giver, the receiver, the gift itself, the timing of the gift), and of cultural and ethical aspects of gift giving. In this way, ESL programs and teachers can help their students understand appropriate U.S. gift giving in general, not just student–teacher gift giving, and thus help students avoid confusion and embarrassment in future situations.

CLASSROOM DISCUSSION OF GIFT GIVING

By putting gift giving in a broad context, instructors can avoid any discomfort that may come from bringing up the subject of students' giving teachers gifts. Discussions and lessons can come out of the classroom material naturally. For example, numerous short stories, television show episodes, and movies have gift-giving scenes. O. Henry's (1906) short story "The Gift of the Magi," and Whitney Otto's *How to Make an American Quilt* (1991), are just two examples. In addition, a teacher can easily find newspaper and magazine advice columns, articles, and advertisements about gift giving. Certain holidays and occasions (e.g., Valentine's Day, Christmas, weddings, graduation) afford excellent opportunities for introducing the topic. Stories, movies, and television shows can also be used to differentiate among gifts, mementos, tokens, and bribes; between appropriate and inappropriate gifts; and among the various gift-giving practices in various cultural groups in the United States and elsewhere (as always, taking care not to overgeneralize about or stereotype any given culture).

These various types of selections can serve as springboards to gift-related vocabulary exercises, problem-solving exercises, discussions, and role-playing scenarios. Questions such as what is considered personal, what is considered expensive, and when a gift might be seen as a bribe would arise naturally in the context of these selections. A sample role-playing scenario might be about a student who enjoys her ESL class and would like to give the teacher a gift at the end of the semester. She knows that other students in the class enjoy the class also, and has heard other students talking about giving the teacher a present. What should she do? Other scenarios could illustrate situations that cause cultural and ethical misunderstandings. Students could role-play a situation where a student and her teacher had socialized outside of class, perhaps going to a lecture or having a cup of coffee together. The student has given the teacher a gift during the semester. Nevertheless, the student's final grade for the semester is a D; she feels that this is a betrayal by the teacher and asks the teacher to raise the grade. Role-playing gift-related situations affords the opportunity for teachers to suggest what would or would not be appropriate gifts in various situations.

These exercises and activities allow teachers to tactfully steer students who want to give teachers gifts toward acceptable and appreciated presents, such as photos of the class, or cards or drawings signed by all the students, rather than more expensive or overly personal gifts. Students are usually curious about gift-giving customs in the United States, and generally have many questions about what to do in certain situations they have faced or may face. What should they take as a gift when they visit an American roommate's parents' home? What should they give a friend or colleague who is expecting a baby? Should they give Christmas gifts even though Christmas is not a holiday they celebrate? As most students are aware that gift giving differs across cultures, they appreciate instructors' helping them to avoid inadvertent cultural or ethical mistakes.

Gift giving should be and generally is a joyful, generous, unambiguously positive gesture and event. However, teachers cannot ignore the classroom situations in which gift giving is, or may be, problematic. It is better for all involved—both teachers and students—to bring the issue out in the open and examine the various aspects of and questions regarding gift giving. Of particular importance is that instructors examine and educate themselves about the cultural and ethical aspects of gift giving as these aspects might relate to classroom experiences. It is also important that ESL professionals share both their knowledge and their questions with their students, and that they do so in a way that draws students into the thinking and decision-making process. As teachers do so, they must ensure that they do not appear to be, and in fact are not, judgmental of differences in culture or of the students and their own gift giving practices.

ACKNOWLEDGMENT

This chapter has been adapted from an article originally published as Messerschmitt, D., Hafernik, J. J., & Vandrick, S. (1997, Winter). Culture, Ethics, Scripts, and Gifts. *TESOL Journal*, *7*(2), pp. 11–14.

PART

THE BROADER CONTEXT

This book is organized into three parts, all dealing with issues ESL faculty encounter as teachers, but each part presents a slightly different emphasis. In reality, the boundaries between the sections are not so clear. Part I of this work, "Inside the Classroom," focused on what happens between faculty and students within the walls of the classroom. Part II, "Outside the Classroom," looked at relationships and activities between faculty and students, largely on campus and within the context of the institution. Part III, "The Broader Context," now expands the focus to include issues that cut across the classroom, the institution, the community, the TESL profession, and society. Taking a broader view of ethical practice reveals that faculty do not operate in a vacuum in spite of considerable academic independence and freedom. Decisions about the administration of ESL programs and the institution have ethical implications for individual faculty members, even though they may be unaware of or have had no input into these decisions. For example, ESL administrators and other institutional leaders routinely make decisions regarding promotional literature, recruitment, admissions, and interpretation of INS regulations. Ethical considerations are inherent in these decisions, and they impact the classroom and faculty, albeit often indirectly.

Because faculty operate within a context and, moreover, because the lines between faculty obligations inside the classroom and those outside the classroom are often blurred, a discussion of the ethical obligations and responsibilities of faculty needs to include broad issues and the broader context. In Part III, we address such issues. Chapter 11 looks at the intersection of program curricular decisions and individual faculty curricular decisions. How are program-wide curricular decisions made? How do they impact individual faculty? What ethical obligations do individual faculty members have to their students, to the program, and to the institution with regard to curriculum? Chapter 12 examines the ethical obligations that faculty have toward the institution and colleagues and supervisors. Do faculty have responsibilities in their interactions with other personnel, and duties in using institutional facilities and representing the institution? What is the balance between obligations that an institution has to faculty and obligations faculty have to an institution? In chapter 13, we take up the topic of faculty research. As more ESL faculty undertake action research and classroom-based research, issues of ethical procedures and responsibility arise. What are the lines between one's research agenda and best practice in the classroom? What criteria can be used to evaluate the benefits of conducting classroom-based research? What safeguards for the protection of subjects are needed? How are individual contributions to research best acknowledged? In chapter 14 we take up the issues of academic freedom inside and outside the classroom. There is much debate within the TESL profession and academe about these issues. Are advocacy and academic freedom related? When does advocacy become coercion? What is the balance between academic freedom and fulfilling one's professional and ethical obligations? Finally, in chapter 15, we address the issues of gender and class. We examine these variables and their impact on the teaching and learning environment.

CHAPTER

11

Curriculum Design and Implementation

Scenario One

At a moderate sized intensive English program (IEP) on a community college campus, faculty as a group chose the textbooks for each class prior to the beginning of the semester. The books were then ordered through the bookstore. At registration, students were given a list of required textbooks that they then purchased. Ms. Oakley had taught at the IEP for several years and had helped in textbook selection each semester. Although she had not objected to the adoption of the book for her oral communications class, after beginning the semester, Ms. Oakley decided that she did not like it. The students had purchased the required textbook and accompanying tape and brought them to class everyday. Ms. Oakley brought in her own material and when asked by the students about the required textbook, she replied that they would be using it occasionally but that the material she brought in was much better. She told students not to return the textbook to the bookstore for a refund. The students were puzzled, as after several weeks Ms. Oakley had not used the required textbook or tape at all. The students liked Ms. Oakley and felt that they were learning, but were confused because they did not know from one day to the next what the lessons would cover and had no way to review material that Ms. Oakley presented in class. A group of students decided to speak to Mr. Lockwood, the IEP director, about the matter. They explained to Mr. Lockwood that they liked Ms. Oakley and her class but wanted to use the textbook that they had purchased. It seemed like a good textbook, and they liked the fact that it had an accompanying tape. They added that it was too late to return the books to the bookstore for a refund.

Scenario Two

A religious young female student, Sister Maria, in an intensive English program on the campus of a religious university, confided in Ms. Norton, one of her teachers, that she was confused by the lessons in Mr. Dayton's oral communications class. Sister Maria was unsure why certain material was being used and what she was learning, if anything. She told of lessons using selections from MTV that she found sacrilegious and offensive, lessons with profanity, nudity, and mockery of religious icons. She said nothing negative about Mr. Dayton per se, but was afraid of approaching him to ask why this material was being used. Sister Maria felt very uncomfortable in Mr. Dayton's class and thought some of the other students did, too. She asked Ms. Norton for advice.

Scenario Three

Miss Jones loved teaching ESL. She worked part time for a private language school, teaching a high level oral communications class each 6-week session. Her schedule was ideal in that she taught in the morning and had her afternoons and evenings to pursue her art career. She was becoming known locally as an artist and had had several private shows. After attending a TESL conference that focused on content and theme-based instruction, Miss Jones decided to add a theme to her oral communications class: art. Students were required to give oral reports on American artists, learn art vocabulary, practice pronouncing art terms, identify slides of specific artists' work, and compile their own art portfolio of original work. After the first 2 weeks, Mr. Morton Thompson, a student in the class, became frustrated and complained to the director of the school, Ms. Pinkerton. He explained that he had saved money to come to the United States to study, had taken 2 months from work as an accountant in an insurance company in Oslo to study English and travel, and that he did not want to "waste his money" studying art.

Central to teaching ESL and to the ESL classroom is curriculum and its implementation. Indeed curriculum is often what one thinks of first when one says "teaching." Questions about the content of the classes, the skills to be covered, the goals, the requirements, and objectives are all questions of curriculum. How much, when, and what types of social justice issues to introduce are also curricular issues. The issues surrounding curriculum design entail much more than deciding on textbooks and objectives. In this chapter, we examine the contexts of curriculum design, ethical and contractual obligations of faculty, freedom that individual faculty members have in making curricular decisions, and working for change within the system.

CONTEXTS OF CURRICULUM DESIGN AND IMPLEMENTATION

ESL programs vary in the amount of freedom individual faculty members have in designing curriculum and choosing materials and methods. Programs and faculty feel both internal and external pressures for students to achieve certain levels of proficiency, and restraints are placed on schools and faculty. Programs have objectives, requirements, and outcomes for each course and level. There may also be standardized or program-wide tests that students are required to pass before advancing in their studies. There may be limits on the amount of time students can be enrolled in ESL courses (e.g., legal restrictions as passed by a state or federal agency, institutional limits), and methods may be dictated (e.g., no bilingual classes, the process approach for teaching writing). Student performance on tests may influence funding, hiring, and curricular decisions. The specific objectives, outcomes, and methods are generally set by the individual program, but may be influenced by the institution, the district, the state, or the federal government. Ideally ESL programs are guided by sound research and by ESL standards developed by TESL and international educational professionals (e.g., the TESOL standards for postsecondary programs, standards set by accrediting agencies such as the Commission on English Language Program Accreditation [CEA]); however, political factors often play a large role in determining objectives, requirements, and other curricular decisions. Another component that guides curricular decisions is social justice. In summary, a multitude of complex factors influence curricular decisions, some directly and others indirectly.

ETHICAL OBLIGATIONS OF FACULTY

Within these contexts, ESL faculty have certain ethical obligations regarding curricular issues as do faculty in other disciplines. Minimally, faculty need to adhere to contractual obligations. Contractual obligations are generally spelled out in written contracts, letters of appointment, and faculty handbooks. Yet, ethical obligations entail more than simply adhering to one's legal obligations. Common ethical considerations fall into a broad category of adhering to guidelines of the program. This means complying with approved and published course content[1] and adhering to the program's course goals, objectives and requirements. By agreeing to teach in an ESL

[1]We use the word "content" here to mean subject matter or skill area. We do not use the word as commonly used in the phrase "content-based instruction."

program, an individual has implicitly agreed to abide by the program's curricular imperatives.

Faculty members' complying with approved and published course titles and content is analogous to the institution's offering the ESL program it publicizes in its catalogues and brochures. For example, if an ESL brochure says that 25 hours of ESL instruction per week are offered, then students must receive 25 hours a week of instruction. As well as publishing general information about the ESL program, school catalogues and brochures generally contain brief descriptions of individual courses. A faculty member assigned a basic level grammar course is ethically bound to teach grammar, not U.S. history or composition. Granted the faculty member can use information from U.S. history in teaching grammar, but the focus is on grammar and on helping students master certain grammatical structures. Granted also that faculty can have students write compositions using targeted grammatical structures. The distinction between teaching U.S. history or composition and using U.S. history and composition to teach grammar may seem small and at times is; however, the distinction is important. Faculty members need to be ever mindful of what the titles and content descriptions of the courses are and to ask themselves if it is clear to the students what the focus of the course is. In Scenario Three, Mr. Thompson seems to have a legitimate complaint. If the focus of Miss Jones' 6-week oral communications class is on art and on students producing art and not on English listening and speaking skills, then Miss Jones is not delivering the promised course. This is not to say that theme-based or content-based courses are by their nature inappropriate, but faculty need to keep in mind the balance between subject matter and language skills. As a next step, Ms. Pinkerton, the ESL director, needs to speak to Miss Jones, allow her to describe her class and her objectives, and ascertain the validity of Mr. Thompson's complaint.

Silva (1997), in his article "On the Ethical Treatment of ESL Writers," echoed the concern for close correspondence of title and course content when he argues that one of the ways teachers need to respect ESL writers is by providing them "with appropriate instruction" (p. 359). One aspect of what he terms appropriate instruction is that students enrolled in writing courses be provided courses that "focus primarily if not exclusively on writing" and that teachers not allow their interests and views, whether they be political or academic, to control or become the curriculum (p. 361).

Other ethical obligations that fall under this general category entail adhering to the program's course goals, objectives, and requirements. These differ from the title and content of the course in specificity, and the degree of specificity varies from program to program. For example, an intensive English program may outline which grammatical structures are to be covered in a basic level grammar class; may stipulate certain textbooks to use; may suggest teaching methodologies, types of exercises to do, and how much homework to give; and may have an in-house exit exam that students must pass to progress to the next level. Similarly in an integrated reading and writing class, the program requirements may specify that students are to keep a weekly journal, practice the process approach to writing (e.g., prewriting, drafting, rewriting, and editing), complete four to six 500-word essays, and read one outside book of 100+ pages.

In Scenario One, Ms. Oakley chose to disregard the textbook assigned to her oral communications class. In addition, she did a disservice to her students by having them buy the textbook which she apparently had no intention of using. A more ethical course of action would have been for Ms. Oakley to have talked to the IEP director, Mr. Lockwood, explaining her objections to the textbook and making her case to use a different textbook or no textbook. Inasmuch as the students had purchased the textbooks and couldn't return them for a refund, the ethical action was for her to use the textbook. Certainly, using supplementary material is appropriate; however, not using the assigned textbook seems unethical. Ms. Oakley can also be more vocal on the textbook selection committee.

A faculty member has the ethical obligation to follow the goals, objectives, and requirements outlined in the program guidelines. Doing this, however, does not mean that the faculty member has no freedom in making curricular decisions for her class or no freedom to work for changes in the set curriculum.

INDIVIDUAL FACULTY FREEDOM IN MAKING CURRICULAR DECISIONS

Within the programmatic curricular guidelines, faculty have considerable freedom. Certain issues are not easily modified by faculty. For example, length of study is one curricular area where individual faculty have little if any freedom. Individual faculty typically cannot decide to add another week of study to a semester/school year or decide to add another hour of in-class instruction to each week, as these are mandated by the state legislature, the school district, the institution, or the ESL program. Similarly, faculty cannot unilaterally decide to change the hour, the classroom, or the day and time of the course. Faculty can propose such changes; however, basic changes such as these are not made easily. Such changes often entail legislative or district approval as well as administrative, and perhaps committee, approval. Such changes also impact others outside the ESL program (e.g., allocation and use of space, transportation services, school organized activities outside of school hours, staff [teaching and nonteaching], families, and students).

Although abiding by the course description and specific guidelines, individual faculty make almost daily curricular decisions regarding such factors as the pace of the course, the amount and type of homework, and number and type of in-class activities (e.g., group work, individual worksheets), use of supplementary materials (e.g., videos, newspaper articles, guest speakers, joint projects with other classes), the kinds and frequency of fieldtrips, the type of grading procedures (e.g., points or letter grades on each assignment, extensive comments on each assignment), and so on.

Let us look at one example in depth. A faculty member has a required text in an advanced business English course that meets 4 hours a week for a 15-week semester. The text integrates the four basic skills and is accompanied by an audiotape and a video. The faculty member decides the order in which to cover the material in the textbook, choosing to skip around and to omit numerous exercises, or even chapters, that she feels are inappropriate for her class. In addition to using the text and the tapes, she regularly brings in newspaper articles from the local newspaper's business section; invites one or two outside speakers to address issues such as international business with Southeast Asia, and U.S. trademark laws; takes her students on one or two fieldtrips to local businesses; and has students research a local company using the Internet and newspapers, then giving an oral and written report to the class. In addition, she decides how much supplementary material to use, how much time to spend on each chapter and activity, how much each assignment counts toward the grade, how many tests to give, what kind of tests (i.e., she must write them), when to give tests, how much and what kind of group work to do, and so on.

This example illustrates the myriad of curricular choices individual faculty have, and highlights questions of ethical practice in faculty choice and use of supplementary as well as required material.

CHOOSING AND USING MATERIALS ETHICALLY

In choosing material, both required textbooks and supplementary material, foremost is the contractual and ethical obligation of faculty members to comply with the course description, goals, and objectives, and to keep in mind that the primary goal of ESL courses is to improve students' English language ability. Other considerations include student characteristics such as age, maturity, educational level, cultural background, needs, and interests. Parental concerns as well as governmental, institutional, and departmental resources and regulations must also be taken into account. Also central is the issue of legality, particularly regarding copyright laws.

Copyright laws and continuing litigation regarding them make it difficult to know exactly what is permissible copying; however, certain copying is obviously illegal. Written into the copyright law is a "fair use" exception to the exclusive right of the owner of the copyright. Copyright laws apply to written material, audiotapes, videos, and broadcast material. Generally school districts, private schools, and postsecondary institutions have written copyright policies. Publisher representatives can also clarify what is legally allowable for their materials. Basically, one can copy limited amounts (e.g., a short selection, a poem, a newspaper article) for one time distribution to students and must not charge students more than the cost of copying. Also notice of copyright should be included on each copy. Repeatedly copying from a particular textbook or using the same copied material each semester is not permissible without written permission from the publisher. If faculty intend to use several parts of a particular text, then students should buy the textbook. Strictly abiding by these basic principles allows faculty to model honesty for students. For example, if an ESL faculty member finds a particularly interesting newspaper article and makes copies for her students, each copy should have appropriate documentation (i.e., title, author, date, newspaper name, section, page, column). Another way to model honesty and teach students about documenting sources is for faculty to tell students where they have found information for the day's lessons. For example, if a faculty member uses an activity suggested by a textbook other than the required one or gives biographical facts about the author of a short story in the required text, she can tell students where she obtained the information or activity and perhaps put the citations on the blackboard. Doing so allows faculty to model and stress the importance of honesty in acknowledging sources.

Institutional resources may also limit the amount and kind of supplementary materials faculty can use. Budgetary restraints may limit the number of available commercial audiotapes, videos, and other material as well as the amount of copying faculty can do. ESL programs, however, often have resource libraries, classroom sets of textbooks, audiotapes, videos, and material files for faculty to use to supplement required texts. Programs may even maintain collective files or notebooks of material for particular classes.

In addition to considering legal and budgetary issues, faculty need to consider student characteristics such as age, maturity, educational level, cultural background, needs, and interests. Units on personal health and health care in the United States are common in ESL courses. In a university ESL program, students may visit the campus health clinic and may have outside speakers as well as cover vocabulary, reading selections, and other material dealing with health issues. Faculty may wish to cover topics such as drinking, drugs, safe sex, and AIDS. Some intensive English programs incorporate a required unit on safe sex and AIDS. Because these are important health topics for students of all ages, the depth and coverage of material will vary according to individual groups. For example, an instructor may decide not to cover issues of personal health with a group of business professionals yet cover them in some depth with young adults in the United States for the first time. Also careful consideration must be given as to how such topics are presented, as different cultural and religious groups and individuals have strong feelings about how, or even if, students should learn about these issues in school or in mixed groups. Student characteristics must also be considered when deciding which social justice issues to cover (e.g., death penalty, abortion, gun control, racial discrimination). In choosing supplementary material, faculty need to be ever mindful of how the material reinforces or expands the language skills being covered. Faculty can choose an additional reading that presents a view different from that presented in the textbook on a topic, can choose a lecture or reading by a minority author not represented in the textbook, can tape a segment of the news that deals with a subject being discussed in class, can use a song that repeatedly uses conditional clauses that are being covered in class, or can use the local public transit map to have students practice reading maps and giving and receiving directions.

The following is an extended example of how a faculty member chose to supplement required material and provide important content for students in her intensive program low-intermediate listening–speaking class. Several students repeatedly had difficulty arriving to her 9 o'clock class because they stayed up late drinking and partying. She feared, and other students confirmed, that these students had alcohol problems. Thus, she decided to supplement the health unit in the textbook by focusing on drinking and drug problems on U.S. college campuses. She brought in articles from the campus newspaper on these issues and had a campus counselor talk to the class about drinking and drugs and available support services. The content was important and appropriate. At the same time, she focused on language and academic skills she had been covering as well: listening to lectures, note taking, asking questions, vocabulary development, and participating in discussions.

Scenario Two raises several related issues: What is appropriate material for a class? Were the MTV clips Mr. Dayton chose appropriate? Did Mr. Dayton have clear academic objectives for the MTV lessons? What actions could Ms. Norton take as Mr. Dayton's colleague? What are Ms. Norton's responsibilities to Sister Maria and to Mr. Dayton? It seems unfair to categorize all MTV or music video clips as inappropriate for ESL classrooms, but profanity, nudity, and mockery of religion are highly questionable at best. Did the clips Mr. Dayton use have these characteristics? At least one student in the class, perhaps more, was not benefiting from the lessons and felt uncomfortable. Such an environment is not conducive to learning English. Mr. Dayton seemed not to have considered the students in his class and how they might be affected by the clips, or to be aware of his students' feelings.

In addition, in this scenario Sister Maria's commenting to Ms. Norton about Mr. Dayton's class places Ms. Norton in a delicate position. She could suggest that Sister Maria speak to Mr. Dayton and explain her confusion and discomfort. However, Sister Maria might feel uneasy doing so. Depending on Ms. Norton's relationship with Mr. Dayton, she could speak to him for Sister Maria, not mentioning names. However, Ms. Norton may not wish to speak to Mr. Dayton as she may fear that he would be defensive or feel that she has no right to question his actions. Another option, but one that should not be taken lightly, is that Ms. Norton could speak to the IEP director and seek her or his advice. If she chooses to do this, she needs to be clear that she has heard from only one student and has not verified Sister Maria's account of the class activities. Whatever decision Ms. Norton makes, it seems that Sister Maria's concerns should be heard, investigated, and addressed, and that Mr. Dayton should have the opportunity to explain his choice of material and actions. If Sister Maria's description of Mr. Dayton's class is accurate, the IEP director should discuss the situation with Mr. Dayton and what is and what is not appropriate class material.

Scenario Two with Mr. Dayton, the extended example earlier of bringing in content on health issues that are affecting students, and the example of Mr. Reynolds, in Scenario One in chapter 3, who received an anonymous complaint from a student's guardian about the content of a reading, highlight the importance of faculty making careful, conscious choices. Curricular choices can promote awareness and understanding of complex social justice issues or can ignore or exacerbate existing problems.

WORKING FOR CHANGE WITHIN THE SYSTEM

In addition to having freedom within their own classroom, ESL faculty can typically address perceived weaknesses in the curriculum and program through approved mechanisms. Recommendations for new courses or changes in existing courses can often be implemented. For example, most ESL programs have a curriculum committee that accepts proposals for new courses or changes in the curriculum. A proposal for a new course outlines specific goals, objectives, and requirements. The amount of detail required varies from institution to institution. The proposal may also need to include a syllabus, with required texts, assignments, number of exams, papers, and other specifics. After receiving the approval of the ESL program, proposals may then need to be approved by an institutional curriculum committee, advisory board, central office or district.

In addition to evaluating course proposals, the curriculum committee, or a subset of it, often serves as the textbook committee. Programs may use different textbooks every year or even each semester, and new ESL materials are constantly published, so evaluation and selection of textbooks are ongoing tasks. In small programs, textbooks may be chosen by the faculty as a whole, and in most programs individual faculty have input into the process. In some programs faculty can choose their own textbooks or choose from an approved list.

The ease in making changes, of course, varies and depends on numerous factors: the type of change advocated, the history of the program, the students, and the work environment. Considering the numerous factors, faculty may need to work collectively and hard to bring about curriculum changes. Of foremost concern should be the responsibility to provide a coherent and effective curriculum for students.

Ideally, before taking a teaching position, faculty ask questions about curricular issues and have a basic understanding of the contractual obligations. Questions might include the following: (a) Are there course objectives, outlines, goals, and sample syllabi? Can I review copies? (b) Are there required textbooks? How are they chosen? (c) Are there restrictions on using supplementary material because of budget or other constraints? (d) Are grades given and, if so, do individual faculty determine how they are computed or are there program requirements? (e) How do students move to the next level (e.g., are there exit exams, standardized tests, teacher recommendations)? With such information, individuals can evaluate how their philosophies and the philosophy of the ESL program match and determine if the program is a place where they would enjoy teaching and could contribute.

CHAPTER

12

Colleagues and the Institution

Scenario One

Having recently arrived in the city, Ms. Boals had been teaching as a part-time member at the local adult school for 3 months. She was doing a good job and seemed well liked by faculty and students. One morning after her classes she asked her supervisor, Mr. Trenton, if he would serve as a reference for her, as she hoped to rent an apartment. She had been staying with friends and was anxious to be on her own. Mr. Trenton asked what information the apartment owner would need. Ms. Boals stated that the owner might call and simply ask if she worked at the institution. Mr. Trenton agreed and informed the teacher that the Human Resources Office could also verify her employment. Mr. Trenton added that he was glad to help. Ms. Boals then stated that she had told the apartment owner that she had worked at the school for a year and requested that Mr. Trenton verify that information if asked.

Scenario Two

Mr. Eagleton was in his second year of teaching at an intensive English program at a land grant university. He was conscientious and carefully prepared each lesson. He had a required textbook for his low-intermediate reading and writing class and often brought in supplementary material. He planned a unit on traffic laws in the United States and other countries. There had been a recent article in the campus newspaper about cameras at intersections on campus and in town used to catch drivers who ran red lights or sped. Mr. Eagleton decided to use this article as a follow-up to a reading selection in the textbook on traffic laws in the United States. He also arranged for a campus police officer to speak to the class on the subject the following week. To begin the unit, he did an exercise getting students to identify vocabulary associated with traffic laws and to talk about traffic laws in their countries and in the United States. Then he asked students to open their books to the appropriate page for the reading on the topic. A student, Jimmy Chong, raised his hand and said, "Mr. Eagleton, we did this reading in our grammar class with Ms. Neilson last week. So, we know all about traffic laws in the United States."

Scenario Three

Ms. Joliet had been teaching at a private language school in a large metropolitan area for almost 10 years. She taught 20 hours a week and specialized in business English and TOEFL preparation courses. Over the last few years, she had become active in a local group working to provide shelter and food for homeless people in the area. She often spent her evenings and weekends distributing food and clothing and lobbying city officials to provide better services for the indigent. She was vocal with her colleagues about her social activism. In addition, at work she regularly faxed information related to the group's activities and frequently duplicated multiple flyers announcing rallies and political meetings.

Scenario Four

Mr. Sullivan loved teaching ESL. He had had part-time teaching positions at three institutions for almost 8 years. He taught 10 hours a week at an intensive English program on a university campus; he taught basic literacy classes to immigrants two nights a week at an adult school; and he taught two composition courses to non-native speakers at the local community college. None of his jobs was near each other and the adult school was more than 40 miles from his house. Despite his three jobs and his hard work, he often had trouble paying his bills and seldom had money or time for a vacation. Halfway through a semester, he was offered more hours at the community college: hours that paid more than either of his other jobs. The new hours, however, conflicted with when he taught at the IEP. Mr. Sullivan knew that a colleague at the IEP, Mr. Jennings, wanted more hours and was available. Mr. Sullivan was sure that Mr. Jennings would be glad to have the additional 10 hours. By taking the additional classes at the community college, Mr. Sullivan could shorten his travel time and increase his income substantially.

Scenario Five

With years of experience teaching English in her homeland, Argentina, Ms. Garcia came to the United States to work on an M.A. in TESL. While doing her graduate work, she had fallen in love and married an American citizen, so she had a permanent resident visa. She graduated with honors and had volunteered at local churches, teaching ESL while completing her degree. Anxious to find a job, she sent her resume to numerous universities, colleges, private language schools, and adult schools in the area. She followed up by calling the director of each ESL program, introducing herself, and asking for an informal interview. She had one interview at an adult school and was offered an evening class teaching Hispanic immigrants. Mr. Allenwood, a director of an intensive English program at a community college, gave her an informal interview. During the interview he informed her that international students wanted native English speakers as teachers and that he had had trouble with non-native English-speaking teachers in the past. Mr. Allenwood also asked Ms. Garcia if she had a U.S. work permit and if she was married and had children. Despite a few awkward questions from Mr. Allenwood, Ms. Garcia thought the interview had gone well, and Mr. Allenwood said that he would contact her if there were openings in the next session that began in 2 weeks. After a month, she had not heard from him. Other ESL program directors indicated that there were no positions available and declined to give her an interview.

Scenario Six

A private language school offered 4-week sessions year-round with 25 hours of instruction per week. The number of classes and levels offered each session was determined by enrollment. Ms. Young had been teaching 15 hours a week at the school for a year and would automatically receive a $3.00 an hour pay raise after teaching for one more session. Ms. Young was consistently rehired and felt she was doing a good job. The first day of the new session, the director, Mr. Polinsky, informed Ms. Young that enrollment was lower than expected and there were no classes for her. Ms. Young was shocked and angry because some teachers hired after her were given classes for the session.

BALANCING FACULTY'S OBLIGATIONS TO THE INSTITUTION AND THE INSTITUTION'S OBLIGATIONS TO FACULTY

Faculty have ethical obligations that go beyond preparing for class, teaching class, and dealing with students. Faculty and their students do not operate in isolation. Typically there are contractual obligations and responsibilities outside the classroom: responsibilities and obligations that directly and indirectly relate to the classroom. In writing of the responsibilities of university professors, Kennedy (1997) stated that "Responsibility suggests the duty one owes to the institution—and, first and foremost, to one's students. . . . In essence, it means delivering full support to a set of institutional objectives" (p. 19).

In speaking of a faculty member's "duty to the institution," one must also consider the institution's "duty to faculty." A faculty member's contractual obligations and responsibilities to an institution and the institution's obligations to her vary from institution to institution and vary according to the type of appointment held. Many ESL faculty, especially in postsecondary ESL programs, are part time and may hold several part-time teaching positions. Like part-time faculty in other disciplines, ESL faculty have little job security, seldom have benefits, and may be paid poorly. National and state professional organizations are currently working on standards for fair employment of ESL professionals, but much work remains to be done. Thus, there is a great deal of variation in working conditions for ESL instructors. Faculty at some institutions are unionized, with contractual obligations and rights clearly outlined. Faculty at other institutions may not have a union contract, but rather a faculty handbook or other printed information detailing what is expected in addition to teaching (e.g., attendance at meetings or in-service training workshops, holding regular office hours, submission of grades and recommendations by a specified date, assistance with administering standardized tests or reading program-wide composition exams). Many of these are considered part of the responsibilities of full-time faculty, whereas part-time faculty may or may not be paid separately for such additional duties. For example, in some programs part-time faculty are paid for attending meetings, whereas in others attendance at meetings is strongly encouraged but not mandatory, or is included in the job description and total pay package. But it would be unusual for faculty to be paid extra for submitting grades or writing recommendations.

Yet even with differences in faculty appointments, all faculty have certain ethical obligations and responsibilities. The most obvious is to fulfill their contractual obligations. Thus, it is very important for faculty to fully understand what they are being hired to do. Before taking a job, ESL faculty, especially part-time faculty, need to ask directly what they are expected to do, if anything, in addition to teaching their classes. Ethically, administrators need to inform prospective faculty of what is expected and not dramatically change expectations after hiring. By accepting the faculty position, one agrees to abide by these obligations.

Typically part-time faculty are hired for a semester or a session with no guarantee of continued employment. Such is the situation of Ms. Young in

Scenario Six. What obligation does the institution have to rehire Ms. Young? The reality is that there is generally no legal obligation for an institution to rehire a part-time faculty member. Enrollments fluctuate and high turnover among part-time faculty is common. Mr. Polinsky may have struggled with the decision not to rehire Ms. Young and considered many factors such as enrollment, job performance, expertise in certain areas, and availability of other faculty. Administrators such as Mr. Polinsky often have little or no control over the terms of faculty employment such as wages, benefits, and maximum number of teaching hours, and may have directives from supervisors that are unpleasant to implement. Mr. Polinsky may have been told by his supervisor not to rehire Ms. Young. Even if the conditions are less than ideal, administrators have an ethical obligation to treat faculty respectfully and humanely. Often administrators actively work to make changes in their programs to benefit faculty. There may be structural impediments to ideal ethical behavior. In such cases, administrators must ask themselves if they can work within the institutional constraints to improve the situation for faculty and students. In the last analysis, administrators have to ask themselves hard questions about their own values and ethics and act upon those values.

Scenario One and Scenario Four also raise questions about the balance between the faculty member's obligation to an institution and the institution's obligation to the faculty member. Does one have less of an ethical obligation to an institution if one feels the institution has little ethical obligation to her? In Scenario One is it appropriate for Ms. Boals to ask Mr. Trenton to lie so that she can get an apartment? Perhaps she feels she is not being paid well, or that because she doesn't have assurances of future employment, Mr. Trenton should do her this favor. It is difficult to imagine a situation where Ms. Boals' request is appropriate and where Mr. Trenton should comply with her request, even if one argues that such a lie has no negative consequences. Scenario Four, however, seems less straightforward. Should Mr. Sullivan leave a teaching position at the IEP midterm for a better position at the community college, or does he have an obligation to complete the term at the IEP? Mr. Sullivan may have no guarantee of future employment at any of the three institutions where he works, may feel the institutions have made little or no commitment to him, yet may be treated very professionally and humanely at each. On the other hand, Mr. Sullivan may feel that he has been exploited, and he may have been. Mr. Sullivan has to weigh several factors: his obligations to his students, his obligations to the IEP, his future employment plans, and his relationships with the administrators at the IEP and the community college. Most important, Mr. Sullivan has to do what he feels is ethically and morally correct. He must weigh all the factors and decide what values are most important to him. If he is on good terms with the IEP administrator, he may wish to discuss his options with her or him or with a close friend who understands his work situations.

Scenarios Four and Six, in particular, highlight issues of social justice toward ESL professionals. Most postsecondary institutions in the United States require a Master's Degree to obtain a TESL position. Yet, often these positions are part time, without job security or benefits. Vandrick, Hafernik, and Messerschmitt (1994) suggested that this may, in part, be due to the predominance of women in the ESL workforce and the fact that many ESL students have little political power. State and national professional organizations strongly advocate more full-time positions for faculty. For example, TESOL has a part-timer faculty caucus that addresses part-time issues and advocates change. While the issue of the working conditions of part-time faculty, in general, is receiving more public attention, progress and change are slow. Part-time faculty in ESL and in other disciplines should be treated with respect and should have good working conditions, decent salaries, and adequate health benefits.

Scenario Five raises questions of hiring and discrimination, another issue of social justice for teachers. Why is Ms. Garcia having difficulty securing ESL teaching positions? Is it because she is a non-native speaker? What questions can employers ask applicants in interviews? The United States Government Department of Fair Employment and Housing publishes a brochure outlining what are acceptable and unacceptable questions to ask applicants. For example, it is acceptable to ask about place of residence, but not appropriate to ask "Do you own or rent your home?" Similarly, it is permissible to ask if the applicant reads, speaks, or writes a language other than English if that information is relevant for the job; however, it is not acceptable to ask questions as to citizenship, nationality, mother tongue, descent, or parentage. Additionally, it is not acceptable for an employer to ask about marital status or the number of children one has. Mr. Allenwood asked several inappropriate questions, showed signs of discrimination, and acted unethically.

Although he cannot say it, Mr. Allenwood was probably correct in assuming that most of his students expected instruction from a native speaker. However, he should consider the positive attributes a non-native speaker could bring to the classroom, including her personal experience in learning English and in this case, knowledge of the specific problem areas Spanish-speaking students encounter in acquiring English. Additionally, he should acknowledge that English is a world language, with different varieties of English considered "standard" in different places. English does not "belong" to individuals in the United States, the United Kingdom, Australia, Canada, New Zealand, and other traditionally English-speaking countries.

FACULTY PRIVILEGES AND CORRESPONDING OBLIGATIONS AND RESPONSIBILITIES

With a faculty appointment come certain privileges and the use of certain resources. Faculty at university or community college ESL programs may have access to the library, discounts at the campus bookstore, reduced fees for use of recreational facilities, discounts for activities and events on and off campus, and so on. For professional use, faculty members are generally provided supplies such as paper, pens, grade books, and computer discs. In addition, faculty may have use of phones, fax machines, copy services, and e-mail. Different institutions define "use" differently. A guiding rule might be that personal use of the phone and e-mail should be kept to a minimum and the use of fax and copying services and supplies should not extend to personal use except in the case of emergencies or with approval of the appropriate administrator. Whereas it seems appropriate to call home to check on a sick child or to make appointments from work occasionally, using the work phone for private consulting or for chatting long distance with friends does not. Similarly, using a grade book and paper from X institution at X institution is appropriate, but not appropriate at another institution. Yet, even with these guidelines, the distinction between professional and personal use is often hazy. Using the program facilities for copying and sending off manuscripts to professional publications, for copying conference handouts, or for making reservations at professional conferences seems appropriate; however, regularly copying one's tax returns or medical records does not.

Perhaps the stickiest area is faculty's use of an institution's supplies and facilities for community projects and other events. Scenario Three illustrates the situation of a faculty member using program equipment and supplies for nonprofessional purposes. Should Ms. Joliet be using the phone, fax, and supplies for her community activism on behalf of the homeless? Ms. Joliet may work hard at the language school, putting in more hours than others; she may be an excellent teacher; she may feel she is underpaid and unappreciated; she may feel that the private language company is financially well-off. Is there a situation that would justify her actions? Is it appropriate to copy flyers for an AIDS march or for a political rally protesting U.S. involvement in a particular country, to fax elected officials requesting they vote for or against certain bills, or to do phone solicitations for a fund raiser for a worthy cause? What if the letter to political officials is regarding funding for ESL programs or financial aid for college students? Questions for individuals to ask are "How does this activity relate to my professional duties? Is there a direct connection between my teaching and this activity or event?" If there is no connection, then it seems inappropriate for the faculty member to use the institution's supplies or facilities. If the connection seems tenuous, then the faculty member can choose not to use the institution's resources or to ask for permission from his or her supervisor to use them. Institutions and programs have limited budgets and, thus, supplies and facilities need to provide the most direct benefit to students and the program as possible. Using program supplies and facilities for personal use may impact the amount of money available for instructional uses.

ETHICAL RESPONSIBILITIES TO COLLEAGUES AND OTHERS

Another ethical obligation is to treat coworkers humanely and with respect. One cannot avoid working with others at the institution: staff, fellow teachers, ESL administrators, and others. Teamwork is especially important in ESL programs, particularly intensive programs, where several teachers generally teach different courses to the same group of students. However, in all ESL programs faculty often collaborate with colleagues planning curriculum, determining programmatic goals, making recommendations and decisions about student placement and advancement, and much more. Collectively individuals can make the program successful, with each person's contribution making the sum greater than the individual parts. However, disagreements among ESL personnel are inevitable and can be healthy: disagreements about student placement, curriculum choices, classrooms, required work, testing, and so on. Differing opinions allow faculty and administrators to examine and evaluate issues and practices closely and to make adjustments as deemed advisable. Arguments and discussions need to be civil and respectful, with individuals remaining open to others challenging their views and with individuals avoiding personal attacks.

Treating colleagues ethically also extends into choices faculty make regarding their classes. Faculty need to be aware of the overall program and how their classes fit into the whole curriculum. Thereby, faculty can choose appropriate supplementary material and activities that enhance their individual class but do not infringe on material and activities in other classes. Communication among faculty is the best way to avoid duplication of material in classes. For example, during a presidential election, faculty often bring in current events about candidates and issues. Such content material could focus on any skill area; however, to avoid faculty using the same material or doing the same type of activities, they should discuss their plans with other faculty who have the same students. A program may wish to have a weekly chart for each level or other organizing device.

In Scenario Two, Mr. Eagleton is naturally surprised to learn that Ms. Neilson has used a chapter from the textbook assigned to his class. This means that the unit Mr. Eagleton planned will have to be substantially revised or not used at all. Did Ms. Neilson not know the textbook was assigned to Mr. Eagleton's class? Is ignorance a good excuse for her actions? How should Mr. Eagleton handle the situation so that this doesn't happen again? Talk to Ms. Neilson directly? Speak to the IEP director? Do nothing? It seems clear that Ms. Neilson should not have used the chapter from Mr. Eagleton's book with her grammar class. If she knowingly did so, it was inconsiderate at the least. How Mr. Eagleton decides to deal with the issue depends on numerous factors: his relationship with the IEP director and with Ms. Neilson, and Ms. Neilson's response when presented with the information. Discussion about curriculum and choice of supplementary material among faculty can minimize the possibilities of such situations arising.

Another issue related to materials and ethical treatment of colleagues is the issue of crediting individuals for material. Often faculty generously share ideas and activities. There may even be a file of supplementary materials that correspond to specific courses. For example, Mr. X may have developed an exercise to accompany a reading selection in the advanced reading text. Thus, when another faculty member teaches that selection, she can use the exercise but should inform students that Mr. X wrote this exercise by insuring that his name is on the handout and by verbally informing students.

Closely related is the issue of acknowledging sources. When using supplementary material faculty need to write the full bibliographical information on handouts and acknowledge sources when giving lectures or information to students. For example, if a faculty member copies an article from the local newspaper, he must be sure to include all the bibliographical information. Similarly, when lecturing, if sources have been used, one should list them. Providing reference information models how students need to learn to credit others and their sources.

Ethical obligations to colleagues, the program, and the institution extend beyond the classroom and the program to the larger institution and the outside world (e.g., the ESL professional community and the local community). Misrepresenting or slandering one's colleagues, program, or institution are obvious examples of unethical behavior. ESL professionals need to make truthful comments about programs, individuals, and institutions based on their knowledge and, ideally, indicate when they do not have adequate information to answer questions. In fact, faculty represent their institution to the ESL profession and larger community, with people making judgments about the program and institution based on individual employees. Thus, an individual's ethical behavior reflects upon one's self, the program, and the institution.

Balancing individual ethical obligations and the institution's obligations to individual employees may at times be difficult. In fact, they may often seem to contradict each other. Administrators and faculty can work with professional organizations and within their institutions to make changes that lead to more humane and respectful treatment of employees by institutions, while striving to make their individual actions as ethical and humane as possible.

CHAPTER

13

Faculty Research

Scenario One

Mr. Withers, a community college ESL instructor, became fascinated by English and Japanese contrastive phonology. He wanted to conduct some independent research. One summer, a perfect opportunity arose when a large group of Japanese teenagers arrived on his campus for a 4-week intensive English class combined with local sightseeing. He decided to study the /l/-/r/ distinction, an area that troubles many Japanese learners of English. Thus, he began the 4-week session by asking each student to read an English passage aloud while he taped it. He also asked each student his or her name at the end of the reading. At the end of the 4-week class he repeated the procedure in order to obtain comparative pre- and postinstructional data. He found some interesting results and immediately began to write a paper to submit for possible publication.

Scenario Two

Professor Bond's research area was speech acts. For his latest project he wanted to look at what native speakers actually say when ordering at a fast food restaurant. Therefore, he requested and obtained permission from the management of a local fast food restaurant to conceal a microphone near the cash register at the counter in order to obtain examples of natural language data.

Scenario Three

Professor Rollins was an assistant professor of applied linguistics at a large state university. In about 2 years, she would come up for promotion and tenure. She already had several single authored publications to her name. She felt that her chances of being successful were good, but she knew she could not be certain. She directed several student research projects, assisting with the conceptualization of the problem and providing guidance along the way, but the students were responsible for all of the work: data gathering, data analysis, data interpretation, and final presentation. Thus, when students submitted articles for publication, Professor Rollins felt it was inappropriate for her to be listed as a coauthor.

Research is a vital human endeavor, necessary for innovation, progress, expansion of the knowledge base, and the betterment of the human condition. It is supported by governments, industry, educational institutions, private donors, and professional organizations. It informs professional practice. For example, research shows that listening comprehension can be taught, and many ESL curricula now devote a substantial portion of time to teaching that skill. Such was not the case 25 years ago when the listening skill was rarely taught in a systematic fashion.

The ethical issues involving research in the field of ESL may not at first seem obvious because they may not seem to be on the same level of seriousness as, perhaps, medical personnel conducting experiments on patients without their knowledge and consent. However, such is not the case. In his work *Genie*, Rymer (1993) cited the example of Psamtik I, the first of the Saitic kings of Egypt, who wanted to find out if there was some type of protolanguage. To that end he devised a simple experiment: "two infants were taken from their mothers at birth and placed in the isolation of a shepherd's hut. The shepherd was instructed not to speak to them. They were thus reared on a diet of goat's milk and silence" (pp. 3–4). According to the ruler's theories, the first words spoken by these babies should have been in the protolanguage. Today, such an experiment would be viewed as child abuse (as was the case of Genie, the abused girl in Rymer's work who was held in a closet with little human contact until puberty).

Such examples, although rare, highlight the need for ethical research. Although the issues involved might not reach the same level of seriousness as those cited earlier, there are several ethical issues in research that must be considered.

CLASSROOM-BASED RESEARCH

Classroom-based research is an activity teachers can and should be involved with. Burton (1998) maintained that "Teachers are central to any reflective process on TESOL research . . . they are uniquely placed by training and practice to provide data on classroom practice . . . and as interpreters of research data they become stakeholders in research outcomes" (p. 419). The classroom contains a myriad of opportunities for academic investigation: projects such as case studies of a single student or observation research on a topic such as male–female language differences.

Classroom-based research necessitates ethical scrutiny. Nunan (1997) asserted that ". . . teacher research must meet the highest ethical standards" (p. 366). Given the nature of our student body, it is critically important that "neither the research or its outcomes be seen to discriminate on the basis of race, ethnicity, gender, sexual orientation, physical disabilities, marital status, color, class, or religion" (p. 366).

Several professional organizations such as College Composition and Communication (CCC) and the American Educational Research Association (AERA) have published guidelines for conducting ethical research. TESOL publishes guidelines for prospective authors submitting articles to their publications in the back of each issue of the *TESOL Quarterly*. In addition, there is a TESOL Research Agenda that includes some limited guidelines for conducting ethical research. Its main thrust is to remind researchers to respect local institutional guidelines. (See Appendix A for a list of professional guidelines, codes of ethics, and useful websites.)

One of the key issues in each of these statements is the protection of human subjects. Davis (1995) noted, "Protecting participants involves guaranteeing that information obtained during the study from and/or about individuals will not be available to others, that is, that anonymity will be ensured" (p. 442). Ideally, any institution sponsoring, supporting, or approving research should have a policy or at least guidelines regarding research. Classroom researchers need to ask themselves questions that fall into three broad categories: protection of the individual; maintenance of appropriate classroom procedures and instruction; and appropriate use, interpretation, and reporting of the data. Note that the first and third group of questions apply to all research done with human subjects whereas the second is particular to research conducted in the classroom. Example questions in each of the three categories follow.

Protection of the Individual

1. Will the participants' anonymity be protected?
2. Will students be placed in any political harm in their native countries or in the United States because of their participation in the research?
3. Will the proposed project treat the participants fairly and equally?
4. Will participation in the project be voluntary?
5. Will participants be able to withdraw at any time without feeling pressured?

Maintenance of Appropriate Classroom Procedures and Instruction

1. How does the project fit in with the overall goals of the class?
2. Will classroom instruction be altered negatively because of the project?
3. Will all participants, those who wish to participate and those who do not, receive the same classroom instruction?

Appropriate Use, Interpretation and Reporting of Data

1. Are the findings and their implications accurately reported?
2. Is the researcher careful not to generalize the findings too broadly?

This list is suggestive, not exhaustive. Professional and institutional guidelines are typically more detailed. Such policies and guidelines are not meant to discourage research, but are intended to help researchers think of ethical responsibilities and the implications of doing research. For example, in classroom-based research, the teacher–researcher must use her power carefully. Students may be reluctant to decline to participate in a project out of fear that a grade might suffer as a result. Every effort must be made to protect students, their time, and their privacy, even if it appears that no harm will result from the research endeavor.

Vandrick, Hafernik, and Messerschmitt (1995) stated that "the researcher must be ever mindful of how writing up the research and the way it is written up may affect students and their lives (e.g., students or their families may be undocumented)" (p. 31). A concern for social justice requires thinking beyond the immediate, seemingly harmless situation and considering the possibility that any research project may actually have some far reaching implications.

In Scenario One, Mr. Withers ignored certain aspects of conducting ethical research, when he used student information and instructional data without students' knowledge or consent. Mr. Withers probably thought the study was harmless. He should have, at a minimum, explained the research project to them, guaranteed their anonymity, and informed them of their right not to participate. These are rights of research participants.

In addition to doing their own research, classroom teachers may be asked to allow their students to participate in research projects conducted by outside researchers, other teachers, or students. Such research might include filling out surveys on attitudes and motivation in language learning, participating in qualitative interview studies, or being videotaped for a study of speech acts. Often these types of research projects are conducted by graduate students completing their degree work. In deciding whether to allow outside researchers to use one's students, faculty need to ask the same questions as with any other research. Questions include the following: Is the research project well designed? Will it take up class time and rob students of instruction? Will students feel coerced to participate? Thus, it is an instructor's prerogative to permit or not permit such research. The decision might be based on how appropriate the instructor feels the research is, how much class time might be needed, how disruptive the project is, and what attempts have been made to assure the students' anonymity. The instructor should check to make sure that the visiting researcher has adhered to the policies of the institution regarding the protection of human subjects. In any case, students must be given the right not to participate, if they so wish. According to the "Ethical Standards of the AERA" (2000),

> Participants, or their guardians, in a research study have the right to be informed about the likely risks involved in the research and of potential consequences for participants, and to give their informed consent before participating in research. Educational researchers should communicate the aims of the investigation as well as possible to the informants and participants (and their guardians), and appropriate representatives of the institution, and keep them updated about any significant changes in the research program. (p. 2)

Nevertheless, there is concern in the field that ESL students may be a particularly vulnerable research population, because some, such as undocumented individuals, have little power. In addition, because these students are still learning English, they may find it difficult to read and understand informed consent procedures. When possible, these procedures should be translated into the students' native languages. If this is not possible, researchers must take extra care to be certain that subjects understand the full extent of their involvement in the research project.

Finally, Professor Bond in Scenario Two, when he wished to obtain natural language for analysis, confronts what Labov (1972) called the observer's paradox. Researchers need examples of natural, spontaneous speech to develop corpora for analyses. However, knowledge of the presence of an observer or a tape recorder may to some extent inhibit a speaker from using natural language, making it difficult to obtain spontaneous speech. How then does a researcher gather spontaneous speech? A researcher such as Professor Bond may be tempted to conceal the recording device in an effort to obtain natural language. Doing so is unethical. This does not mean that Professor Bond must give up his research interest and project. One possible solution is for him to post a sign at the counter informing customers that their interactions are being recorded and stating that they are free to ask that the recording device be turned off. For other research needs where a corpus of natural language is required, a researcher can ask permission to record and, if granted, record a lengthy portion of the interaction so that, with time, the interlocutors may begin to ignore the microphone and speak freely. The crucial point is for individuals to be informed that they are being recorded so that if they wish, they can decline to participate in the research.

ACKNOWLEDGING OTHERS' CONTRIBUTIONS

Finally, another area of ethical concern in research is one of giving credit where credit is due. Research today is increasingly collaborative in nature. Collaboration may be among colleagues, among classroom teachers and university researchers, or among faculty and graduate students. Such collaboration often evolves because the nature of problems today is complex and multifaceted. Thus, the work is best done with input from several different researchers. It is critical that researchers value and acknowledge each other's contributions. Unfortunately, most individuals in higher education know of instances where a senior faculty member or researcher failed to give appropriate credit to a junior faculty member or a graduate student. At best, it may be explained as an oversight, but such oversights must be guarded against. Usually acknowledging the contributions of others enhances the overall project and does not detract from the stature of the primary investigator. It is simply ethical behavior. In Scenario Three, Professor Rollins, when she declined to be listed as a coauthor, adhered to AERA guidelines regarding intellectual ownership. In her position of power as a faculty member, she could have put pressure, however slight, on the students to add her as a coauthor, but she did not. According to AERA guidelines, "It is improper to use positions of authority to appropriate work of others or claim credit for it. In hierarchical relationships, educational researchers should take care to ensure that those in subordinate positions receive fair and appropriate authorship credit" (p. 3). Thus, Professor Rollins' decision seems appropriate.

Finally, students' contributions to the research product must be acknowledged. If students' comments or writings are used, care must first be taken to obtain their permission to use their work. Next, if the student gives permission for the work to be used, does she or he wish to be acknowledged or remain anonymous? Whichever decision a student makes, it must be respected by the researcher.

As this discussion shows, the issue of ethical behavior with regard to research is complex. It is better to be overly cautious in this area than careless. Most educational institutions have strict guidelines for conducting research. As well as possibly harming students, faculty who violate ethical research guidelines could negatively influence their professional standing and jeopardize accreditation standards, with serious consequences. However, following guidelines for ethical research is generally not a cumbersome procedure, and, those interested in conducting meaningful research should not be deterred from doing so. After all, it is from research that one gains insight and new knowledge that may then translate into improved educational practices.

CHAPTER

14

Academic Freedom

Scenario One

The ESL faculty had been evaluating and revising the program's curriculum and orientation program. They had surveyed faculty as well as students to determine what basic information was important to include. Based on the results of the surveys and comments, the ESL faculty agreed as a group to incorporate certain topics (e.g., health issues, safety issues, introduction and orientation to campus facilities such as the library and computer labs) into the regular classes throughout the semester instead of trying to cover them all in 1- or 2-day workshops at the beginning of the semester. One faculty member who had taught in the program for many years, Ms. Lightener, argued vehemently against the idea. After much discussion, the consensus of the faculty was to have one area addressed in each class so that the topics would fit logically with the appropriate classes and so that no faculty member had to take class time to address all the topics. For example, the reading and writing instructor would do a unit on the library and take students on a tour of the campus library, whereas the listening instructor would cover health issues and visit the campus health center. Faculty estimated that none of the prescribed units would take more than three or four class periods and that faculty could work the units into their regular classes as they felt was best. Ms. Lightener refused to cover any of the topics in her class, saying that her academic freedom would be violated if she were required to cover certain material in her class. She insisted that academic freedom gave her the right to teach whatever she wanted.

Scenario Two

Mr. McCormick enjoyed teaching ESL at the local adult school. He had taught U.S. history for many years in the local high school and had gotten his M.A. in TESL so that he could work with immigrants. He felt it was important to help immigrants adjust to life in the United States and to become active in politics by becoming citizens and by voting. Having a good command of English was essential, he felt, to being able to participate fully in life in the United States. With the approval of his supervisor, he had developed a theme-based ESL course for high level students that dealt with the U.S. Constitution and the Bill of Rights. Students liked his class and Mr. McCormick placed special attention on freedom of speech and freedom of the press. He frequently brought in newspaper articles and TV news clips about politics. He was critical of U.S. immigration policies, and especially the position taken by the U.S. President. He made his disapproval of these policies and of the President known to his students. Upon learning of the U.S. President's scheduled visit in the area, Mr. McCormick told his students of his plans to join a demonstration opposing proposed changes to U.S. immigration laws. He invited students to join him in the protest, offering them extra credit for doing so. He believed that their participating would help them become integrated into U.S. culture and would allow them to practice their English.

Scenario Three

Mr. Bowles, the IEP director informed one of the faculty members, Ms. Adams, that she would not be rehired the next semester as she was not performing well in the IEP as indicated by low teaching evaluations for the past two sessions. Ms. Adams had been aware that her evaluations were problematic because Mr. Bowles had had several conversations with her about them and about how to improve her teaching. Despite Ms. Adams' efforts, however, she continued to receive low teaching evaluations. Ms. Adams was upset about not being rehired but soon began looking for other teaching positions. She mentioned to a colleague, Mr. Young, that she was not being rehired and her colleague was surprised and outraged. Mr. Young taught the same students as Ms. Adams and in class one day informed the students that Ms. Adams was not being rehired. He went on to tell the students how wrong this was, asked the students to write letters to the IEP administrator, Mr. Bowles, protesting this action, and handed out sample letters.

Academic freedom is a concept with a long history in U.S. postsecondary institutions. The popular notion of academic freedom is based on the 1940 Statement of Principles and Interpretive Comments on Academic Freedom and Tenure that was jointly created by the American Association of University Professors (AAUP) and the Association of American Colleges (AAC). The freedoms delineated include the freedom to teach, research, publish, and to speak extramurally (Poch, 1993, p. iii). Along with these freedoms come certain faculty responsibilities and obligations, namely to abide by professional and ethical standards of behavior. Thus, without fear of losing her job, a professor teaching a U.S. politics class can argue that Johnson's policy in Vietnam and Bush's foreign policy were detrimental to U.S. domestic affairs and foreign relations. Another politics professor may argue the opposite in her class. Similarly, an English literature professor can introduce feminist writers (e.g., Nawal Al-Saadawi, Kate Chopin, Charolotte Perkins Gilman, Virginia Woolf) and feminist analysis of characters in traditional works (e.g., Shakespeare, Milton, Greek tragedies) or, indeed, design courses in women's literature. Such actions are seen as an academic prerogative and often as a professional and moral responsibility. Academic freedom does not, however, allow faculty to disregard their basic responsibilities to cover the course material, and to create an environment conducive to learning and intellectual inquiry. For example, it is generally inappropriate for a faculty member to use class time to expound on her political views if they are unrelated to the course material (e.g., a chemistry professor probably has no academic reason to discuss the strengths and weaknesses of various presidential candidates in her class).

In Scenario One, the faculty have agreed upon additional material to be covered in each class, thereby adding to the objectives and content of the course. Faculty were not told exactly how or when to cover the topics and could work them into the existing curriculum. Even though Ms. Lightener may disapprove, this decision does not violate her academic freedom. Academic freedom does not give her the right to refuse to teach material agreed upon by the program faculty and administrators. In addition, she is not being asked to teach a particular political or social viewpoint; she is simply being asked to cover a particular topic (e.g., safety issues) that would benefit her students and that could easily be incorporated into her existing course.

Closely tied to the concept of academic freedom and academic responsibility is the concept of advocacy. "Advocacy" has a negative connotation for some who argue that instructors need to present disinterested knowledge, truth, and objectivity (Himmelfarb, 1996). Individuals may argue that a balanced approach to a subject is desirable, with both sides of any argument presented equally. Others argue that faculty are inherently advocates.

> It is incumbent upon us to recognize that advocacy in the classroom with or without political implications is part of the nature of the academy. . . . Let us work toward mutual respect and remember that advocacy is our modus operandi and does not preclude civility. (Friedl, 1996, p. 59)

Following this line of reasoning, ESL faculty who present a unit on AIDS (e.g., what it is, how it is transmitted, how to lessen individual risks of contracting it) are advocating individuals' taking responsibility for their own health and safety (i.e., practicing abstinence, safe sex, and not using dirty needles). Similarly, faculty who present units on the environment in most cases advocate individuals' taking personal steps to lessen humans' detrimental impact on the environment (e.g., encouraging recycling, taking public transportation, consuming less). Presenting a certain position does not mean that faculty do not allow disagreement or that they do not at times explain arguments for opposing positions.

Difficulties arise in defining *advocacy* and in delineating the limits. What is the line between teaching and indoctrination? Between advocacy and teaching? Between advocacy and indoctrination? Between advocacy and proselytizing? The lines between these concepts are blurred even more by issues of authority and power. Faculty have authority and power; thus their actions and statements carry more weight with students than comments from others not in those positions. Having this authority requires that faculty take their positions and authority seriously, acting with responsibility and accountability. Markie (1996) outlined four conditions for appropriate advocacy in teaching:

> (1) allow us to teach the prescribed course content; (2) allow us to create and maintain an environment conducive to intellectual inquiry; (3) remain within the limits of our expertise; and (4) take the form of giving students, for their own assessment, adequate evidence for our position. (p. 298)

He contends that each is required for advocacy to be appropriate. Lunsford (1996) recommended seeing faculty roles "not in terms of a binary between advocacy and nonadvocacy but in relation to the both/and nature of teaching: a sense of advocacy that encompasses a teacher's rights and responsibilities, a teacher's advocacy and accountability" (p. 433).

These issues of faculty rights and responsibilities and faculty's advocacy and accountability are particularly important for ESL instructors. Unlike in the past (e.g., the days of the audiolingual method), today language is viewed as a means of communication, with content seen as an important vehicle for providing language instruction and practice. The primary focus of ESL courses remains helping students acquire sufficient language skills to pursue their goals (e.g., enter a degree program in an English-speaking academic setting; use English in the workplace, or in international professional situations; or use English for personal reasons). Today language instruction, however, is seldom seen as divorced from content. With content-based instruction more widespread in ESL settings, the question of what content or topics faculty choose becomes important. Often program guidelines dictate which language skills or objectives should be covered, but may not prescribe specific content. ESL faculty often develop courses, units within courses, and supplementary materials on various topics of their choice to accompany required textbooks. In this respect ESL faculty may have more freedom as regards content than faculty in other disciplines (e.g., introductory biology, U.S. history, accounting, psychology). ESL faculty can often develop units in content areas or courses in which they are particularly interested (e.g., U.S. films, poetry, the Civil Rights movement in the United States). In choosing content and topics, ESL faculty need to be sensitive to cultural and linguistic diversity in their classrooms and to their particular institutional setting. For example, a topic that is appropriate for a diverse group of ESL students may not be appropriate for a homogeneous group of students. Similarly, what is an appropriate topic at a large public university in an urban area may not be as appropriate at a small religious college in a rural area.

In Scenario Two, Mr. McCormick chose a seemingly appropriate topic for a theme-based course: the U.S. Constitution and the Bill of Rights. Along with language skills, he was teaching concepts important for immigrants in the United States. Yet urging students to accompany him to a demonstration against the U.S. government seems coercive. Perhaps, unintentionally, Mr. McCormick has put them in an awkward position. Because of his position and power, students might not feel comfortable in refusing to attend the demonstration. They may not want to go to the demonstration, but at the same time they might not want to offend Mr. McCormick or risk getting a lowered grade.

Another example of a faculty member's putting students in an awkward position is seen in Scenario Three in which Mr. Young encouraged students to write letters to the IEP director protesting a colleague's not being rehired. Mr. Young's actions seem coercive. In such a situation, were students comfortable refusing to do what he asked? Some students may have felt that Ms. Adams should not be rehired, others may have felt indifferent to her plight, and still others may have agreed with Mr. Young that she was being treated unfairly. Even those who felt she was being treated unfairly may not have felt comfortable protesting the decision in writing. Mr. Young seems to have done a disservice to Ms. Adams also in that he did not ask her if she wanted him to make public her not being rehired, to protest her not being rehired, or to urge students to write protest letters. When students ask for advice on how to make a complaint or disagree with a decision, the most ethical action is to inform students of their options. For instance, if a student wishes to protest a course grade, and asks a faculty member how to do this, the faculty member should provide clear information, outlining the student's rights. But in this scenario, Mr. Young used his power and authority in an attempt to rally support for his position.

A final related concept is that of balance. One argument for balance within a course would go as follows: An instructor doing a unit on the English-Only Movement in the United States would present the arguments for each side objectively without taking a position, thus providing a balanced view. But Lunsford (1996) and others argued that the goal should be "balance" across the curriculum, not within a given course, that faculty should be able to advocate a position, presenting arguments and counterarguments for the position. Striving for balance of perspectives across an ESL curriculum entails discussions among faculty, not agreement among faculty. Faculty need not agree about the English-Only Movement or agree on particular films to study in a U.S. film course. ESL faculty are in an ideal position to have discussions about content and curricular issues. When such conversations are respectful and civil, both faculty and students benefit.

The interactions among academic freedom, advocacy, faculty obligations, and faculty accountability are complex and often context dependent. They impact faculty and students in myriad ways and cannot be ignored.

CHAPTER

15

Gender and Class

Scenario One

Hyun Park was a serious young student who attended a private language school in the Midwestern United States. She came to her ESL class every day and always did her homework, but rarely participated in class discussions. She only spoke when the teacher called on her, in contrast to several of the male students who were quite spontaneous and vociferous in expressing their opinions in class, often even interrupting others who were talking. However, Hyun was always very attentive; she sat forward on her seat, followed the conversation with obvious interest, and often nodded when others spoke. When given writing assignments, particularly journal writing, she expressed her ideas and feelings well, sometimes even passionately, about a wide variety of topics.

Scenario Two

In Ms. Staubach's intermediate level IEP class, the topic of homosexuality came up as one of the issues addressed in an assigned reading on civil rights for various groups. Immediately some of the young men in the class laughed, and some made gestures imitating stereotypes about gay men's behavior, such as limp-wristed waves. In the ensuing discussion, other students stated that "homosexuality is wrong," and still others stated that there were no homosexuals in their country. During this exchange, one student, Juan Cortazar, was very quiet and seemed to shrink into his seat.

Scenario Three

Mr. Bertrand taught at a private university with high tuition. One day before an advanced ESL writing class got started, several students and the teacher were chatting about various topics. Ahmed Al-Kasri was clearly excited and told his classmates that his father had just bought him a brand new car, the car he had always wanted, a Mercedes convertible. He stated that he had "finally" (at the age of 19) gotten the car of his dreams. Some classmates congratulated him and joked about his giving them rides. Others were silent; some of them had obtained loans or scholarships in order to attend the university, and some were working many hours a week just to pay for their tuition. These students had no cars, or drove old and distinctly nonluxury cars. Mr. Bertrand himself thought ruefully of his own battered 11-year-old Ford Escort that would very soon need a new transmission as well as new brakes.

Ethical treatment of students includes faculty's being aware of students' backgrounds, or possible backgrounds. As discussed in chapter 7, students' social and political backgrounds can affect what they bring to the classroom, what they are concerned about in the classroom, and how they are treated by other students in the classroom. There are a number of other factors in students' backgrounds and lives that also affect what they bring to the classroom and how they are perceived and treated (by faculty as well as by other students) in the classroom. Two of the most important of these are gender and social class. Both gender and class are complicated by cultural factors. Crucial considerations in dealing with gender and class issues include, first, how to ensure that all students, of whichever gender or class, are treated ethically and fairly, and second, how to guide students to think about these issues in ways that expand their understanding and enhance respectful treatment of others, yet respect their own beliefs and cultural values. These considerations are the focus of the discussion here.

GENDER

Although the ways in which males and females have been treated differently have changed with time, especially since the early 1970s, there are still significant differences in the ways that females and males are brought up and regarded. In general, parents and society still have somewhat different expectations and aspirations regarding the education and careers of females and males. And these differing expectations by parents and society influence the expectations and aspirations that young people have for themselves. This is true in the West, and perhaps even truer in many non-

Western countries. Female students in ESL classes, just by virtue of being in English classes, often in a different country, may not be representative of females from their countries. They are likely to come from families that allow more freedom for, and have higher ambitions for, their daughters than other families in their countries may allow. Yet these women students still, often, do not feel as comfortable in classes as their male counterparts do, and they are still, often (though generally unconsciously), treated differently by faculty.

There has now been about 30 years of research about the different experiences of female and male students in educational settings. Research set in the United States indicates, in summary, that females receive less attention from teachers than males do; females are often sexually harassed in schools; adolescent girls and young women tend to lose confidence in their academic abilities, especially in science and math; girls and young women benefit from single-sex schools; females work better cooperatively than competitively in classroom situations; and girls and young women need female role models and mentors (AAUW, 1992, 1998; Pipher, 1994; Sadker & Sadker, 1994; Sandler, Silverberg, & Hall, 1996).

There has been far less research about gender differences specifically in ESL settings. The limited research indicates that some ESL materials have been sexist; female and male language learners sometimes have different learning styles; and ESL programs and classrooms are not always conducive to female students' learning (Pavlenko, 2001; Porecca, 1984; Schenke, 1996; Sunderland, 1994, 1995, 1998; Vandrick, 1994, 1998). Schwarte (2000), President of TESOL at the time she wrote, called for more research on gender issues in ESL teaching, as did Vandrick (1999b) and others.

Some scholars have suggested that the classroom situation (in general, not specifically for ESL) has actually become much better for females, and that now it is time to turn our attention to the needs of males in school. These scholars state that the classroom environment is actually more favorable to females' learning than to males' learning, and that female students on average receive higher grades in school. Although this argument may have some merit, it underestimates the problems that female students still have. It also does not give enough attention to intragender differences, such as those between female students of different ethnic and economic backgrounds (AAUW, 1998). In any case, educators need to pay attention to the needs of all their students, female and male; to do so they need to be aware of the research and pay careful attention to what is going on in their own classrooms, watching for gender differences, and differential treatment of females and males, and thinking of ways to address these issues.

In considering ESL pedagogy, where the focus is on language use, questions of differing language use by women and men, especially as they relate to student behavior and to pedagogical issues, are of particular interest. Linguists such as Lakoff (1975, 1990), Kramarae (1981), Spender (1980), Tannen (1996) and Cameron (1990) have found the following about the ways women and men speak and communicate: Women use politer and more tentative language, male speech is the *norm* and female speech is seen as deviation, women are labeled and discussed in patronizing and demeaning ways, and the English language uses specific conventions (e.g., the generic "man" and "he") which marginalize females. Although some of these differences and problems may be lessening after three decades of feminism and changes in society, language does not change quickly, and these matters are still a concern. ESL teachers should be aware of such language issues and watch for their effects; further, such language issues are useful and appropriate topics for class discussion.

FEMINIST PEDAGOGIES

Based on the kinds of research discussed earlier, many educators have developed a loose constellation of pedagogical approaches that can be labeled *feminist pedagogies*. These pedagogies are influenced by, and overlap with, critical pedagogies. Critical pedagogues believe that education is always influenced by politics and ideology, that education is much more than teaching facts and information, and that critical thought can lead to transformation. Feminist pedagogues agree with these principles, and add that

> education has been structured in a way that perpetuates male dominance, and . . . that attention must be paid to the needs and learning styles of females, as well as to the problems of sexual harassment and stereotyping that harm female students. (Vandrick, 1999a, p. 9)

Whether or not they choose to label one's pedagogy as feminist, many ESL teachers will note that the principles of feminist pedagogies are those of equity, ethics, and social justice (see McMahill, 1997; Vandrick, 1995b).

The first challenge, regarding both equitable treatment in the classroom and, closely related, equitable language use in the classroom, is to ensure that females and males are treated ethically and fairly in ESL classrooms. Teachers can first make themselves aware of the research, and the issues, in general. Next, they can examine their own teaching and their own classrooms on these issues. Some teachers have found it useful to videotape one or two of their own classes and then watch the videotape with an eye for how often they address or engage male students and female students, how much female students and male students are engaged with the class material and with each other during discussions, and what students' body language says about their comfort level and involvement with the class.

Because female students' participation may be less vocal but just as attentive as male students', teachers can, first, give credit for less vocal participation and, second, design classroom activities so that all students can participate in their different ways. For example, in some cases female students will be more likely to participate in small group discussions than in whole-class discussions. Or they may be more likely to discuss class topics freely in a journal entry or other written format than to speak out during class. Hyun Park, in Scenario One, for example, is a student whose participation might be overlooked by some teachers, and who might even be graded down for "not participating," when in fact she is very involved with the class and is participating in many ways, but not in the traditional way of speaking out frequently during class discussions. Teachers need to look out for students such as Hyun and notice their participation. Note too that such "noticing" on the part of teachers will benefit not only female students but also other students who feel less comfortable speaking out, such as shy students, students who are first-generation college students, and any other students who may not feel at ease vocally establishing their place in the academic setting.

The second challenge is to expose students to issues regarding gender, and to help them work their way through these issues, thinking about their own backgrounds and values, and thinking about any new information and ideas they encounter in class, not only from the readings and other class materials but also from their classmates and teachers. This process can be integrated smoothly into class curricula, complementing and supporting the ways in which gender-related topics fit students' academic and language needs. As well as needing to know about these issues for reasons of social justice, students will find that these topics are now increasingly discussed in various disciplines that they will encounter in their academic studies (e.g., sociology, politics), and that discussing these issues in their ESL classes will help to prepare students for further academic classes. One extended example of focusing on a female-oriented topic can be found in Benesch (1998). Benesch's EAP class, linked to a college psychology class, focused partially on the topic of anorexia, in an attempt to add diversity to the psychology class curriculum, which included very little material related to women's psychology. Students in this EAP class learned about feminist and psychological analyses of anorexia, at the same time enriching and supporting their learning of psychology, and psychological vocabulary and conventions.

Fortunately, there have been some clear changes regarding gender roles and expectations in recent years, around the world. In classes at the university level in the United States, the proportion of women has increased substantially. For example, according to a recent *Open Doors* report, from 1976/1977 to 1997/1998, female students increased from 30.8% to 41.1% of the international students studying in the United States (Institute of International Education, 1997/1998). When females are not in a definite minority, but represent nearer to half the class, they gain strength from each other, and they are much more likely to participate actively in class discussions and other activities; they are much more likely to express their opinions with confidence. Also many of today's young women, in many countries, have been raised with higher educational and career expectations than in the past. In particular, young women who come from privileged backgrounds are likely to have been given the best of everything, and are likely to expect to continue to receive the best of everything, including educational and career opportunities. (This of course raises issues of social class as well, demonstrating the intersections of gender and class in educational and other settings.)

An important issue related to that of gender is that of sexual identity. Many people find it extremely difficult to discuss the issue of homosexuality (or bisexuality or transgender). Yet most of the same ethical and social justice concerns apply to this issue as apply to issues of female and male identities. First, all students, whatever their sexual identities, should be treated ethically, fairly, and respectfully in class. Second, when issues regarding homosexuality—or related issues, such as AIDS, that often become the stimulus for discussion of homosexuality—are raised in class materials or discussion, all opinions should be expressed respectfully. Whether or not there are gay or lesbian students in a given class (and note that Juan, in Scenario Two, may have been gay), it is important to act as if there were; in other words, it is important to express one's opinions with respect and thoughtfulness. Ms. Staubach, the teacher in Scenario Two, needed to make this point tactfully but clearly and firmly to her students, especially regarding the mocking of gay people. This is not to say that students with views that are negative about homosexuality should not be allowed to express them, but simply to say that discussion should be on a level of respect. And there may be cultural and religious factors that influence students' views on this topic. These need to be respected as well. But often students' views are based on ignorance or on opinions they have absorbed without really thinking about them. When students such as those in Scenario Two make comments such as "Homosexuality is just not acceptable in my country (or culture)," or even "There are no homosexuals in my country," there is an opportunity for probing of these statements, for providing information, and for helping students clarify the real reasons for their opinions. Many of the classroom activities mentioned earlier regarding gender issues can also be used or adapted to focus on sexual identity issues.

FEMINIST ETHICS

Drawing together issues of gender and ethics, there is now a new area of study entitled "feminist ethics." Feminist ethics, broadly described, maintains that there is an ethic of care, springing at least partially out of a maternal ethic, and a special concern on the part of women, especially mothers, with the feelings of others. Feminist ethics is also situated in ". . . the explicitly political perspective of feminism, wherein the oppression of women is seen to be morally and politically unacceptable" (Sherwin, 1993, p. 16). Sherwin also pointed out that feminist ethics includes the belief that "the morally relevant features of any decision making situation include the agents' responsibilities to specific persons, including themselves" and the belief in "the significance of rooting ethical decision in specific contexts and thus rejecting traditional ethical theory's commitment to purely abstract reasoning" (p. 18). This is not a call for moral relativism, but a reminder that people should consider the very real details of very real lived experiences when making moral decisions. The tenets of feminist ethics are most famously outlined in Gilligan (1982); Noddings (1984); and Young (1990); see also Card (1991); and Clement (1996). The assertion that an ethic of care is more often found among females than among males is of course controversial. But whether or not one agrees that females are more inclined to a particular approach to people and to ethics, one can see the value in the ethic of care. Therefore it is useful to have a field of studies, feminist ethics, which explores questions of gender and ethical decision making.

CLASS

Class, meaning social class, is a concept widely understood around the world, and quite codified in many parts of the world. In the United States, class is much less widely discussed, and in fact is often treated as a concept that is not very relevant in U.S. culture (Vandrick, 1995a). This is partly because of the democratic basis of the United States, and the consequent need for the country to see itself as completely egalitarian. Even when it is admitted that some people are more privileged than others, there is the belief that one's position in society is up to the individual; if one works hard, one can be successful and climb to a higher class. In addition, for some North Americans there is an association of the concept of class with Marxist/communist analysis, which is anathema to most Americans, thus providing another reason to avoid recognition of and mention of social class. But in fact there is a class system in the United States, just as there is elsewhere, even when it is seldom alluded to.

This class system is as evident in academe as elsewhere. Students of working-class backgrounds often suffer, feeling that they are disadvantaged by not knowing the ways of academe, and not having the resources needed for success. There is also sometimes an element of shame, as such students feel they need to hide their backgrounds and attempt to "pass" as middle-class. Soliday (1999) pointed out that

> Working-class students' struggles to gain and sustain access to the 'cultural means of production' create educational life narratives that sharply differentiate them from their bourgeois counterparts. The number of hours worked and various family responsibilities are correlated strongly with both the type of institution that these students attend and their retention rates. (p. 734)

She further pointed out that working-class students often have to deal with "[r]emedial courses and other institutional hurdles" (p. 734) and that they often take longer to complete their degrees, and she urged that we "examine and challenge the barriers the academy places in the way of working-class students" (pp. 737–738).

The issue of class is present in the ESL classroom as elsewhere. Often this manifests itself through economics: It becomes clear that some students, such as Ahmed, who is given a Mercedes for his 19th birthday, in Scenario Three, come from privileged backgrounds and have access to ample funds for education, expensive cars, designer clothes, and frequent travel. Others in the same classroom may be struggling to pay tuition, perhaps working two jobs, and have little money left over for luxuries or even what most would consider basics. It also becomes clear that some students come from families high up in the social systems of their home countries, whereas others do not. Although all are currently focusing on getting an education, some do so as a natural, assumed next step; others do so as a difficult, precarious step. Privileged students may convey a sense of entitlement, or may be condescending, which may well be resented by less privileged students. Privileged students may also take so much for granted that they are heedless and tactless in the assumptions they make, again perhaps causing resentment in other students; such resentment may well have been felt by Ahmed's classmates in Scenario Three.

Social class differences may be especially noticeable when there are students from the same country or ethnic background, but of different social classes, in the same classroom. People are generally particularly attuned to the (sometimes subtle) class distinctions made in their own countries or cultures, and may be more likely to judge other people from their own cultures in terms of class than they would so judge people from other cultures. One clear-cut example of discrimination on the basis of class is that of the situation of an underclass, even outcast, group in Japan, originally scorned because of their jobs as butchers, known as the "burakumin." Reischauer (1977) referred to the burakumin as "a sort of outcast group" and states that "social prejudice against them is still extreme . . . most Japanese are loath to have contact with them and are careful to check family records to insure that they avoid intermarriage" (p. 36). Some members of this class are now able to move toward the middle class in Japan and even study abroad. However, discrimination persists today in such areas as marriage, employment, real estate sales, and education (Domoto, 2000) and students will almost never publicly admit that they are of the burakumin group, as they are quite sure that their fellow Japanese in an ESL class or program will shun them if they know of their identity. Students from other underclass groups in other countries may suffer similar fears of discrimination even when studying abroad.

As with gender, there are two facets of ethical treatment of class issues in the classroom. One is to treat all students with respect and ensure that all students treat each other with respect. Sometimes signs of disrespect may be subtle and impossible to monitor, such as some students' casually overlooking or acting superior to poorer or less well-dressed or less sophisticated students. But even when teachers cannot completely control such behavior, they need to help students become aware of the implications of their behavior.

Education is the second facet of ethical treatment: Issues of class can be addressed directly or indirectly, through class materials and discussion. Acknowledging that class divisions exist is the first step. Discussing their implications is the second. Teachers may seek out specific readings and other materials that raise issues of class. Mitchell (1996/1997) showed concern about the absence of references to class in writing textbooks, stating that

> even those based on difference tend to deal only marginally with the issue of social class . . . few examine the institution of class itself, much less the means by which favored classes use government and other institutions, even our beloved academy, to perpetuate themselves. (p. 70)

Mitchell goes on to recommend readings on class that would be suitable for composition or other classes; some of these would certainly be suitable for use in advanced ESL classes. Another way to address class issues is through reading and discussing fiction, probably short stories, that address social class (Solomon, 1999, is one collection of such stories). Getting at the issues of privilege and class through literature allows a focus that does not personalize the matter within the classroom, unless a student or teacher herself chooses to volunteer relevant personal information or perspectives. Literature also has a particular power to make the consequences of class divisions very real, very believable. It encourages readers to make the imaginative leap that allows them to grasp the perspective of another, and it is this imaginative leap of understanding that is necessary before one can change one's thinking and behavior.

CONCLUSION

Although teachers cannot single-handedly rectify injustices and inequities in society, such as those often experienced by females and by members of nonelite classes, they can be aware of the ways in which gender and class can affect students' lives, including their experiences in the classroom. Whether such inequities consist of blatant discrimination or of more subtle manifestations of differential treatment, teachers can be watchful and proactive in noticing problematic areas and in guarding against them or countering them as much as possible.

CHAPTER

16

Conclusion

Ethics are at the very core of human existence; humans throughout history have wrestled with questions of ethics in various arenas: marriage and family, child rearing, education, the workplace, politics, the law, war and peace, the arts, and more. One could make an argument that the area of education is one of the most important of these, one which affects all the other areas. Educators thus have a unique and enormous responsibility to use their positions wisely and to ascertain and act upon their ethical principles.

However, teachers are generally so busy with preparing classes and actually teaching that they have little time to focus on questions of ethical dilemmas. This is not to say that teachers do not call upon their ethics and values, and apply them as needed in the classroom and other places. But because they are busy, they may not have time to dwell on these issues or even think about them until a crisis or other difficult situation arises. In addition to the problem of time, there is the issue of anxiety about discussing ethics and ethical issues with others. Because teachers know that their colleagues may have at least slightly different ethical beliefs than they do, they may prefer not to risk being judged negatively, and not to risk raising uncomfortable and perhaps controversial topics such as whether a given teacher's behavior is "right" or "wrong." Because of this silence, teachers in training may not get the preparation they need to think about these difficult topics ahead of time. New teachers may encounter complex and difficult situations they are not prepared for, and even experienced teachers may struggle with issues alone rather than realize that others are probably dealing with the same issues, and others can help. This silence does not stop teachers from making decisions, because they must deal with these dilemmas. Teachers may not take the time to ask themselves what their guiding values and ethical principles are, how they can and should be applied, and what complicating factors should be taken into consideration. In addition, teachers may not make the time and take the initiative to discuss ethical concerns with colleagues.

The way that humans make ethical decisions is informed by history, religion, philosophy, culture, the law, institutions, and personal experience. Most people develop their own senses of what is ethical and what is not. But when asked to articulate these systems or guidelines, most people have difficulty. Complicating the matter is the difficulty of applying guidelines to specific, complicated, sometimes unique situations. There is always a play between principles and practice. This is not to say that there are no universal or overarching principles, but to say that in real-life situations, even such principles may not provide enough guidance to give unambiguous answers regulating people's actions.

It is because of this difficulty that we, in this book, problematize, struggle with, and try to articulate the kinds of issues and the kinds of decision-making processes that teachers need to think through and work through. We hope that our mutual engagement, as authors and readers, with this process, as well as our mutual engagement with the dilemmas set out in the scenarios we outline, will be of use to readers as they deal with their own individual situations in their own classrooms. We hope that in this book we have illustrated the ways in which ethical dilemmas and decisions infuse almost every aspect of the teaching of English as a second language. We hope too that we have shown how a focus on social justice can provide a framework and guidance for classroom teachers faced with making ethics-related decisions.

Furthermore, we would like to call for increased attention to matters of ethics in the field of teaching ESL. We urge that readers discuss these issues with their colleagues, speak about them at meetings and conferences, and write and publish about them in professional arenas. If both individuals and professional organizations focus more than heretofore on issues of ethics and social justice, the conversations we as ESL professionals have together can make a real difference to our students, our colleagues, our profession, and the world.

APPENDIX

A

Professional Guidelines, Codes of Ethics, and Useful Web Sites

American Educational Research Association. (2000). *Ethical standards of AERA*. Retrieved September 18, 2000, from the World Wide Web: http://www.aera.net/about/policy/ethics.html

California Teachers of English to Speakers of Other Languages (CATESOL). (1995, January 28). *CATESOL position statement on distance education for non-native learners of English*. Orinda, CA: Retrieved April 5, 2001, from the World Wide Web: http://www.catesol.org/disted.html

Center for the Study of Ethics in the Professions. Illinois Institute of Technology. http://csep.iit.edu/codes/codes.html

College Composition and Communication. (2001). Guidelines for the ethical treatment of students and student writing in composition studies. *College Composition and Communication, 53*, 485–490.

Linguistic Society of America. http://www.lsadc.org/web2/resolutionsfr.htm

Modern Language Association of America. (No date). *Statement of professional ethics*. New York: Modern Language Association of America.

NAFSA: Association of International Educators. (2000). *Code of ethics*. Washington, DC: NAFSA Publications. Retrieved April 27, 2001, from the World Wide Web: http://www.nafsa.org

National Education Association. (No date). *Code of ethics of the education profession*. Washington, DC: NEA. Retrieved June 19, 2000, from the World Wide Web: http://www.near.org/aboutnea/code.html

TESOL (2000). *TESOL Research Agenda, June 2000*. Retrieved January 30, 2001, from the World Wide Web: http://www.tesol.org/assoc.bd/006researchagenda01.html

TESOL Informed Consent Policy Statement and Release. Retrieved July 8, 2000, from the World Wide Web: http://www.tesol.org/pubs/author/consent.html

APPENDIX

B

Additional Scenarios

Included are additional scenarios to stimulate thought and discussion. All ESL teachers have similar stories.

Scenario One

Miss Seegers taught an intermediate conversation class at a large IEP. She was a relatively new teacher and wanted her students to like her. Unfortunately, one of her students, Mr. Yoshi Abe, talked in class continually, day after day. Miss Seegers said nothing until one day in the middle of the semester, Mr. Abe laughed and began pulling on his classmate's moustache. His classmate, Mr. Juan Gonzalez from Mexico, was surprised and not amused. Miss Seegers was, by now, totally exasperated and asked Mr. Abe to leave the class. Although he looked surprised, he did so. He did not return for the remainder of the semester.

Scenario Two

Miss Li Park was majoring in English at her university in Korea. She planned to teach after graduating. During a holiday break she and her fiancé got married. When she returned to her studies, she once again had Mr. Brown as her teacher for Advanced Conversation. Because he had also been her instructor for Intermediate Conversation, she felt fairly comfortable talking to him. But when she told him that she had gotten married over the break and was now Mrs. Kim, all he said was, "Well, I sure hope you don't get pregnant this semester."

Scenario Three

Ms. Lisa Cohen noticed that one of the students in her adult school beginning level class, Ms. Leah Salvatori, often came to class with bruises on her face and body and often wore sunglasses indoors. In addition, Leah had a discouraged look and posture. She was in her early 30s and was married. One day Ms. Cohen drew Leah aside privately and asked her about her injuries. At first, Leah was silent, and then, she began weeping and said that her husband had been beating her off and on for months, and that she didn't know what to do about it. She didn't have money or resources to leave him, and she was afraid that even if she did leave, he would find her and harm her.

Scenario Four

Abdul Al Thani, a young student from the Middle East who was in the United States for 3 months to study English at a private language school, often carried large amounts of cash and did not make much effort to hide it. His teacher, Ms. Ellen Bradbury, cautioned him that his cash might draw the attention of pickpockets, muggers, or other criminals. Abdul said he could defend himself and seemed unconcerned.

Scenario Five

Mr. Takeshi Mori raised his hand to ask about the meaning of an obscene gesture he had seen while riding with some friends. He demonstrated the gesture several times. Ms. Brown, his teacher, had a feeling that he already knew the meaning and was simply testing her and the class.

Scenario Six

Miss Tashi, an experienced community college ESL instructor, did not appreciate having Mr. Alvaro Gomez in her intermediate writing class. He was somehow, very strange, and she couldn't quite put her finger on what the problem was. In any case, she was actually happy when he was absent, which was fairly often. One morning, however, he walked into class just after she had begun passing out the exams, and, without saying a word, began undressing in front of the class.

Scenario Seven

A small intensive English program worked hard to create a friendly, welcoming atmosphere where students, administrators, faculty, and staff knew each other. The IEP office and all the IEP classes were in the same building.

Around the middle of one semester, a young man, a stranger to the IEP, came into the IEP office hurriedly. He said that he was a good friend of Amelia, an IEP student, and asked where he could find her. The IEP staff member told him the room number where Amelia was in class.

Scenario Eight

Considered an excellent teacher, Mr. Harolds had been teaching literacy and ESL at the local adult school in a large urban area for several years. As a single parent, teaching daily from 9 o'clock until 12 o'clock allowed him to have his daughter, Amy, in preschool in the mornings and to spend his afternoons with her. His colleagues as well as the office staff knew and liked Amy as he often brought her into the office in the afternoon when he needed to complete work for the next day's classes. One morning at 8:45, Mr. Harolds and Amy arrived in the ESL office. Mr. Harolds explained that Amy had a cold and was running a low fever. Because he could not find a babysitter and Amy's preschool would not allow her to attend if she had a fever, he asked if the office staff could let her stay with them while he taught his classes. Mr. Harolds proceeded to make Amy a bed on the floor in the back corner out of the way. He promised to look in on her between classes.

Scenario Nine

Like other faculty, Ms. Dunlap, a part-time faculty member in a university ESL program, regularly received examination copies of ESL textbooks from publishers. She, of course, adopted the ones she felt were most appropriate for her classes. About once a year an individual came to the university offering to buy unused examination copies. Needing the money, Ms. Dunlap regularly sold her desk copies to this individual who then sold them to students at much below the publishers' prices.

Scenario Ten

Isabel Hernandez was a student at an intensive English program in a small university town. She requested to live with an American family. The IEP referred students to a reputable homestay program company that was developed to serve the IEP's needs. Isabel was placed with the Jensen family: a mother and father, two teenage children, and a dog. Isabel liked living with the Jensens at first as they included her in family dinners and outings, making her feel like one of the family. After about 2 months, however, she began to feel uncomfortable in the Jensens' house and dreaded being with them. Religion was very important to the Jensens. They had Bible readings at breakfast and an hour of Bible reading and prayer each evening after dinner. The Jensens expected Isabel to participate in these activities as well as to attend church with them twice on Sundays and one weekday evening. At first, Isabel did not mind these activities because she thought they would help her improve her English quickly. But the Jensens became more insistent that she be "saved" and join their church. They made derogatory remarks about Catholics, Jews, Muslims, and other religious groups. Isabel was afraid to tell them that she was Catholic and did not hold the same religious beliefs that they did. She also wanted to move to another homestay, but at the same time did not want to hurt the Jensens' feelings as overall they had been very kind to her. She asked Mr. Kerry, her writing teacher, for advice.

Scenario Eleven

Marta Holbeck, an advanced IEP student from Europe, hoped to complete her program and begin her undergraduate degree the next semester. The Intensive English Program had an agreement with the university that students who successfully completed the highest level of IEP courses would be admitted to the university as matriculated students. Marta was doing fairly well in her classes except for Ms. Oakley's writing class. It was obvious to Ms. Oakley that Marta's overall English ability was better than that of most of the other students in the class. In addition, Marta wrote well as evidenced by her performance on the in-class compositions and exams. She, however, was frequently absent, having missed more than one third of the classes, and had submitted only 1 of the 6 required out-of-class essays. The last day of class when students were to submit their portfolios, Marta handed in hers with five essays and a rewrite of the one that she had handed in earlier in the semester. Marta's portfolio was better than the other students' and Ms. Oakley was confident that Marta had done the work herself. Ms. Oakley felt that Marta could handle university classes, yet felt uncomfortable giving Marta a good grade in the class.

Scenario Twelve

Mr. Lee was a relatively new teacher at a language school that attracted international students for short-term programs combining travel and study. He came highly recommended from his graduate advisor and had been a Teaching Assistant while earning his MA in applied linguistics. Mr. Lee was a U.S. citizen and his first language was Korean. He was eager to do a good job and help his students enjoy their stay in the United States, so he planned his lessons very carefully. After 1 week, several students in the class complained to the director, Ms. McBride that they couldn't understand Mr. Lee. They demanded a refund, claiming they had assumed they would have a native English speaking teacher.

Scenario Thirteen

Shortly after the semester began, Ms. Gould, the director of an adult school, received two separate student complaints about Ms. Craven's arriving late to class and her not being prepared. Ms. Gould was troubled by these complaints because several students had written similar comments on Ms. Craven's evaluations the semester before. Ms. Gould decided to investigate and began asking Ms. Craven's students and other teachers if Ms. Craven arrived to class on time, if she was well-prepared, if she returned papers promptly, and so on. Ms. Gould's probing questions made students and faculty uncomfortable.

Scenario Fourteen

Mr. Mifflin had been teaching at the university IEP for several semesters and was hired to teach in a short-term summer program for Japanese college women. The women were excited about their first trip to the United States and were eager to experience U.S. culture. The women liked Mr. Mifflin as his lessons were always interesting and he accompanied them on after-class excursions such as going to the movies or out for pizza. One day after class, Mr. Mifflin invited three of the young women over to his apartment to go swimming. He told them that he would like to take pictures of them at the swimming pool and in his apartment. The young women were confused about what to do; one said that they were busy that afternoon. The next day, they decided to ask Ms. Rigby, their grammar teacher, what they should do if Mr. Mifflin invited them again.

Scenario Fifteen

Ms. Mercer was an experienced teacher and was generally successful at getting every student to participate. One semester seemed particularly difficult as her grammar class had mostly quiet Asian students and several vocal Europeans. She made sure to call on every student so that each one could have a chance to practice orally, but this meant that sometimes she had to ask other students to remain quiet. The Asians tended to have a better grasp of the grammatical concepts than the other students but were more reticent to speak. One day after class Olaf Borg came to her office and said that he wanted to be moved to another class as he was better than everyone else and none of the Asians could speak or knew any English. She explained to him that actually most of the Asians had a better command of English grammar than he did and that they were simply not as talkative as he was. Ms. Mercer denied his request to move to another class. About an hour later, Naoki Mori came to Ms. Mercer's office and requested to move to another class because some of the students were too aggressive in the grammar class. Noaki went on to make the argument that Europeans and Asians should not be in the same ESL classes as Europeans never allowed Asians to speak and were arrogant.

References

American Association of University Women (AAUW). (1992). *How schools shortchange girls.* Washington, DC: AAUW Educational Foundation.

American Association of University Women (AAUW). (1998). *Gender gaps: Where schools still fail our children.* Washington, DC: AAUW Educational Foundation.

American Educational Research Association. (2000). *Ethical standards of AERA.* Retrieved September 18, 2000 from the World Wide Web: http://www.aera.net/about/policy/ethics.html

Bellah, R. N., Madsen, R., Sullivan, W. M., Swidler, A., & Tipton, S. M. (1985). *Habits of the heart.* New York: Harper and Row.

Benesch, S. (1998). Anorexia: A feminist EAP curriculum. In T. Smoke (Ed.), *Adult ESL: Politics, pedagogy, and participation in classroom and community programs* (pp. 101–114). Mahwah, NJ: Lawrence Erlbaum Associates.

Birch, B. (1992, June/July). ESL peaceteachers. *TESOL Matters, 2,* 11.

Birch, B. (1993). ESL techniques for peace. *The CATESOL Journal, 6,* 7–15.

Bishop, W. (1997). *Teaching lives: Essays and stories.* Logan: Utah State University Press.

Bloch, J. (2001, February). *Intellectual property in the L2 classroom.* Paper presented at the 35th Annual TESOL Convention, St. Louis.

Bromley, H., & Apple, M. W. (Eds.). (1998). *Education/Technology/Power: Educational computing as a social practice.* Albany: SUNY Press.

Burak, P. A., & Hoffa, W. W. (Eds.). (2001). *Crisis management in a cross-cultural setting* (2nd ed.). Washington, DC: NAFSA Publications.

Burton, J. (1998). A cross case analysis of teacher involvement in TESOL research. *TESOL Quarterly, 32,* 419–446.

California Fair Employment and Housing Commission. (1993). *Pre-employment inquiry guidelines.* Sacramento, CA: California Fair Employment and Housing Commission.

California Teachers of English to Speakers of Other Languages (CATESOL). (1995, January 28). *CATESOL position statement on distance education for non-native learners of English.* Orinda, CA: Author. Retrieved April 5, 2001 from the World Wide Web: http://www.catesol.org/disted/html

Cameron, D. (Ed.). (1990). *The feminist critique of language: A reader.* London: Routledge.

Card, C. (Ed.). (1991). *Feminist ethics.* Lawrence: University Press of Kansas.

Chapelle, C. A. (Ed.). (2000). TESOL in the 21st century [Special issue]. *TESOL Quarterly, 34,* 3.

Christison, M. A., & Stoller, F. L. (1997). *A handbook for language program administrators.* Washington, DC: NAFSA Publications.

Clement, G. (1996). *Care, autonomy, and justice: Feminism and the ethic of care.* Boulder, CO: Westview Press.

Coffey, M., & Grace, S. (1997). *Intercultural advising in English-language programs.* Washington, DC: NAFSA.

College Composition and Communication. (2001). Guidelines for the ethical treatment of students and student writing in composition studies. *College Composition and Communication, 53,* 485–490.

Connor-Linton, J. (1995). Looking behind the curtain: What do L2 composition ratings really mean? *TESOL Quarterly, 29,* 762–765.

Curran, C. A. (1972). *Counseling-learning; A whole-person model for education.* New York: Grune & Stratton.

Currie, P. (1998). Staying out of trouble: Apparent plagiarism and academic survival. *Journal of Second Language Writing, 7,* 1–18.

Dalai Lama. (1999). *Ethics for the new millennium.* New York: Riverhead Books.

Davis, K. A. (1995). Qualitative theory and methods in applied linguistics research. *TESOL Quarterly, 29,* 427–453.

Domoto, M. (2000). The Buraku situation. Retrieved May 24, 2001 from the World Wide Web: http://www.uncc.edu/imedomoto/3209/minorities/buraku.html

Egbert, J., & Hanson-Smith, E. (Eds.). (1999). *CALL environments: Research, practice, and critical issues.* Alexandria, VA: Teachers of English to Speakers of Other Languages (TESOL).

Egbert, J., Chao, C.-C., & Hanson-Smith, E. (1999). Computer-enhanced language learning environments: An overview. In J. Egbert & E. Hanson-Smith (Eds.) *CALL environments: Research, practice, and critical issues* (pp. 1–13). Alexandria, VA: Teachers of English to Speakers of Other Languages (TESOL).

Fox, H. (1994). *Listening to the world: Cultural issues in academic writing.* Urbana, IL: National Council of Teachers of English

Fox, L. (1992, February/March). Doing peace education: Getting started. *TESOL Matters, 2,* 7.

Friedl, E. (1996). Choosing voices. In P. M. Sparks (Ed.), *Advocacy in the classroom: Problems and possibilities* (pp. 51–59). New York: St. Martin's Press.

Gilligan, C. (1982). *In a different voice: Psychological theory and women's development.* Cambridge, MA: Harvard University Press.

Giroux, H. (1992). *Border crossings: Cultural workers and the politics of education.* New York: Routledge.

Greenblatt, S. (1999). Advising students facing a political crisis at home. *International Educator, 8,* 23–26, 52.

Hafernik, J. J., Messerschmitt, D. S., & Vandrick, S. (2000). Safety Issues for International Students in the United States. *TESL Reporter, 33*(2), 1–9.

Hafernik, J. J., Vandrick, S., & Messerschmitt, D. S. (1999, June/July). Incorporating safety issues into IEPs. *TESOL Matters, 9,* 15.

Hamp-Lyons, L. (1998). Ethical test preparation: The case of the TOEFL. *TESOL Quarterly, 32,* 329–337.

Hamp-Lyons, L. (1999). Comments on Liz Hamp-Lyons' "Ethical test preparation practice: The case of the TOEFL": The author responds. . . . *TESOL Quarterly, 33,* 270–274.

Harris, R. (2000). Anti-plagiarism strategies for research papers. Retrieved August 4, 2000 from the World Wide Web: http://www.vanguard.edu/harris/antiplag.htm

Hatch, E. (1992). *Discourse and language education.* New York: Cambridge University Press.

Hawisher, G. E., & Selfe, C. L. (Eds.). (1989). *Critical perspectives in computer and composition instruction.* New York: Teachers College Press.

Hawisher, G. E., & Selfe, C. L. (Eds.). (1999). *Global literacies and the World Wide Web*. New York: Routledge.

Henry, O. (1906). The gift of the Magi. In *The four million* (pp. 16–25). New York: A. L. Burt.

Himmelfarb, G. (1996). The new advocacy and the old. In P. M. Sparks (Ed.), *Advocacy in the classroom: Problems and possibilities* (pp. 96–101). New York: St. Martin's Press.

Howard, R. M. (1995). Plagiarisms, authorships, and the academic death penalty. *College English, 57,* 788–806.

Institute of International Education. (1997/1998). Profiles: Field of study and sex by nationality. *Open doors report.* Retrieved March 13, 2001 from the World Wide Web: http://www.opendoorsweb.org/Lead%20Stories/Profiles.htm

Johnston, B. (in press). *Values in English language teaching.* Mahwah, NJ: Lawrence Erlbaum Associates.

Johnston, B., Juhász, A., Marken, J., & Ruiz, B. R. (1998). The ESL teacher as moral agent. *Research in the Teaching of English, 32,* 161–181.

Kast, R. C. (1997/1998, Fall/Winter). Liability issues in international studies programs. *International Educator, 7,* 27–32.

Kelly, C. (2001, January/February). Less can be more—Simple can be elegant: Designing web sites. *ESL Magazine,* pp. 12–13.

Kennedy, D. (1997). *Academic duty.* Cambridge, MA: Harvard University Press.

Kibler, W. L. (1994). A comprehensive plan for promoting academic integrity. In R. B. Axelrod & C. R. Cooper (Eds.), *The St. Martin's guide to writing* (pp. 257–260). New York: St. Martin's Press.

Kidder, R. M. (1995). *How good people make tough choices.* New York: William Morrow.

Kohl, H. (1994). *"I won't learn from you" and other thoughts on creative maladjustment.* New York: The New Press.

Kramarae, C. (1981). *Women and men speaking: Frameworks for analysis.* Rowley, MA: Newbury.

Kubota, R. (1999). Japanese culture constructed by discourses: Implications for Applied Linguistics research and ELT. *TESOL Quarterly, 33,* 9–35.

Kuehn, P., Stanwyck, D. J., & Holland, C. L. (1990). Attitudes toward "cheating" behaviors in the ESL classroom. *TESOL Quarterly, 24,* 313–317.

Labov, W. (1972). *Sociolinguistic patterns.* Philadelphia: University of Pennsylvania Press.

Lakoff, R. (1975). *Language and woman's place.* New York: Harper and Row.

Lakoff, R. T. (1990). *Talking power.* New York: Basic Books.

Lee, H. M. (2001). *Reflection on controversial topics in ESL classes.* Unpublished manuscript. University of San Francisco.

Leki, I. (1992). *Understanding ESL writers: A guide for teachers.* Portsmouth, NH: Boynton/Cook.

Linguistic Society of America. http://www.lsadc.org/web2/resolutionsfr.htm

Lionnet, F. (1995). *Postcolonial representations: Women, literature, identity.* Ithaca, NY: Cornell University Press.

Lunsford, A. (1996). Afterthoughts on the role of advocacy in the classroom. In P. M. Sparks (Ed.), *Advocacy in the classroom: Problems and possibilities* (pp. 432–437). New York: St. Martin's Press.

Machan, T. R. (1997). *A primer on ethics.* Norman: University of Oklahoma Press.

Markie, P. (1996). The limits of appropriate advocacy. In P. M. Sparks (Ed.), *Advocacy in the classroom: Problems and possibilities* (pp. 293–302). New York: St. Martin's Press.

McMahill, C. (1997). Communities of resistance: A case study of two feminist English classes in Japan. *TESOL Quarterly, 31,* 612–622.

Messerschmitt, D., Hafernik, J. J., & Vandrick, S. (1997, Winter).Culture, ethics, scripts, and gifts. *TESOL Journal, 7*(2), 11–14.

Mitchell, J. P. (1996/1997). Money, class, and curriculum: A freshman composition reading unit. *Writing on the Edge, 8*(1), 67–76.

Modern Language Association of America. (No date). *Statement of professional ethics.* New York: Modern Language Association of America.

Monroe, C. (1991, June/July). Too busy to care anymore: Burnout and the ESL program administrator. *TESOL Matters, 1,* 17–18.

Morrison, T., Conaway, W. A., & Borden, G. A. (1994). *Kiss, bow, or shake hands: How to do business in sixty countries.* Holbrook, MA: Bob Adams.

Moskowitz, G. (1978). *Caring and sharing in the foreign language class: A sourcebook on humanistic techniques.* Rowley, MA: Newbury House.

Murray, D. E. (1991). *The computer terminal as medium of communication.* Amsterdam: John Benjamins.

Murray, D. E. (1995). *Knowledge machines: Language and information in a technological society.* London: Longman.

Murray, D. E. (1996, August/September). Technology is driving the future . . . Part II. *TESOL Matters, 6,* 3.

Murray, D. E. (2000). Protean communication: The language of computer-mediated communication. *TESOL Quarterly, 34,* 397–421.

NAFSA: Association of International Educators. (2000). *Code of ethics.* Washington, DC: NAFSA Publications. [Available online]. http://www.nafsa.org

National Education Association. (No date). *Code of ethics of the education profession.* Washington, DC: NEA. [Available online]. http://www.near.org/aboutnea/code.html

Noddings, N. (1984). *Caring: A feminine approach to ethics and moral education.* Berkeley: University of California Press.

Nunan, D. (1997). Developing standards for teacher-research in TESOL. *TESOL Quarterly, 31,* 365–367.

Nussbaum, M. C. (1999). *Sex & social justice.* New York: Oxford University Press.

Otto, W. (1991). *How to make an American quilt.* New York: Ballantine.

Palattella, J. (2001, March). May the course be with you. *Lingua Franca,* 50–57.

Pavlenko, A. (2001). Bilingualism, gender, and ideology. *International Journal of Bilingualism, 5*(2), 117–151.

Pennington, M. (1991). *Building better English language programs: Perspectives on evaluation in ESL.* Washington, DC: NAFSA Publications.

Pennington, M. (1996). *The computer and the non-native writer: A natural partnership.* Cresskill, NJ: Hampton.

Pennycook, A. (1994). The complex contexts of plagiarism: A reply to Deckert. *Journal of Second Language Writing, 3,* 277–284.

Pennycook, A. (1996). Borrowing others' words: Text, ownership, memory, and plagiarism. *TESOL Quarterly, 30,* 201–230.

Pipher, M. (1994). *Reviving Ophelia: Saving the selves of adolescent girls.* New York: Putnam's.

Poch, R. K. (1993). *Academic freedom in American higher education: Rights, responsibilities, and limitations.* Washington, DC: The George Washington University, School of Education and Human Development.

Porreca, K. L. (1984). Sexism in current ESL textbooks. *TESOL Quarterly, 18,* 705–724.

Rea-Dickins, P., & Germaine, K. P. (1999). *Managing evaluation and innovation in language teaching: Building bridges.* New York: Longman.

Reischauer, E. O. (1977). *The Japanese.* Rutland, VT & Tokyo: Charles E. Tuttle.

Rymer, R. (1993). *Genie.* New York: Harper Perennial.

Sadker, M., & Sadker, D. (1994). *Failing at fairness: How America's schools cheat girls.* New York: Scribner's.

Safety in study abroad: ¿Como no? (1998). *International Educator, 7,* 54–57.

Sandler, B. R., Silverberg, L. A., & Hall, R. M. (1996). *The chilly classroom climate: A guide to improve the education of women.* Washington, DC: National Association for Women in Education.

Schäffner, C., & & Wenden, A. L. (Eds.). (1995). *Language and peace.* Aldershot, England: Dartmouth.

Schenke, A. (1996). Not just a "social issue": Teaching feminist in ESL. *TESOL Quarterly, 30,* 155–159.

Schneider, A. (1999, January 22). Why professors don't do more to stop students who cheat. *Chronicle of Higher Education,* pp. A8–A10.

Schneiderman, S. (1995). *Saving face: America and the politics of shame.* New York: Knopf.

Schwarte, B. (2000 October/November). What does TESOL stand for? *TESOL Matters, 10,* 3–4.

Scriven, M. (1982). Professorial ethics. *Journal of Higher Education, 53,* 307–317.

Seward, J. (1972). *The Japanese.* New York: William Morrow.

Shats, L. (1994). *The difference between American and Ukrainian high schools.* Unpublished manuscript, University of San Francisco.

Shen, F. (1989). The classroom and the wider culture: Identity as a key to learning English composition. *College Composition and Communication, 40,* 456–459.

Sherwin, S. (1993). Ethics, "feminine ethics," and feminist ethics. In D. Shogan (Ed.), *A reader in feminist ethics* (pp. 3–28). Toronto: Canadian Scholars' Press.

Silva, T. (1997). On the ethical treatment of ESL writers. *TESOL Quarterly, 31,* 359–363.

Smith, P. (1994). Cheating in the ESOL classroom: A student-centered solution. *TESOL Journal, 4,* 51.

Soliday, M. (1999). Class dismissed. *College English, 61,* 731–741.

Solomon, B. (Ed.). (1999). *The haves and have-nots: 30 stories about money and class in America.* New York: Signet.

Spack, R. (1997). The rhetorical construction of multilingual students. *TESOL Quarterly, 31,* 765–774.

Spender, D. (1980). *Man made language.* London: Routledge & Kegan Paul.

Spender, D. (1995). *Nattering on the net: Women, power, and cyberspace.* North Melbourne, Australia: Spinifex.

Sterba, J. P. (1998). Introduction. In J. P. Sterba (Ed.), *Ethics: The big questions* (pp. 1–18). Malden, MA: Blackwell.

Sunderland, J. (Ed.). (1994). *Exploring gender: Questions and implications for English language education.* Englewood Cliffe, NJ: Prentice Hall.

Sunderland, J. (1995). Gender and language testing. *Language Testing Update, 17,* 24–35.

Sunderland, J. (1998). Girls being quiet: A problem for foreign language classrooms? *Language Teaching Research, 2*(1), 48–82.

Tannen, D. (1996). Researching gender-related patterns in classroom discourse. *TESOL Quarterly, 30,* 341–344.

Taylor, T. W., & Ward, I. (Eds.). (1999). *Literacy theory in the age of the Internet.* New York: Columbia University Press.

TESOL (2000). *TESOL Research Agenda, June 2000.* Retrieved January 30, 2001 from the World Wide Web: http://www.tesol.org/assoc.bd/006researchagenda01.html

United Nations. (2000). Beijing+5 process and beyond. Retrieved March 27, 2001, from the World Wide Web: http://www.un.org/womenwatch/daw/followup/bfbeyond.htm

Vandrick, S. (1994). Feminist pedagogy and ESL. *College ESL, 4*(2), 69–92.

Vandrick, S. (1995a). Privileged ESL university students. *TESOL Quarterly, 29,* 375–380.

Vandrick, S. (1995b). Teaching and practicing feminism in the university ESL classroom. *TESOL Journal, 4*(3), 4–6.

Vandrick, S. (1997). The role of hidden identities in the postsecondary ESL classroom. *TESOL Quarterly, 31,* 153–157.

Vandrick, S. (1998). Promoting gender equity in the postsecondary ESL class. In T. Smoke (Ed.), *Adult ESL: Politics, pedagogy, and participation in classroom and community programs* (pp. 73–88). Mahwah, NJ: Lawrence Erlbaum Associates.

Vandrick, S. (1999a, February/March). Who's afraid of critical feminist pedagogies? *TESOL Matters, 9,* 9.

Vandrick, S. (1999b, April/May). The case for more research on female students in the ESL/EFL classroom. *TESOL Matters, 9,* 16.

Vandrick, S., Hafernik, J. J., & Messerschmitt, D. S. (1994, Spring/Fall). Outsiders in academe: Women ESL faculty and their students. *Journal of Intensive English Studies, 8,* 37–55.

Vandrick, S., Hafernik J. J., & Messerschmitt, D. S. (1995). Ethics meets culture: Gray areas in the postsecondary ESL classroom. *The CATESOL Journal, 8*(1), 27–40.

Vandrick, S., & Messerschmitt, D. (1997–1998). The web of classroom exchanges. *The CATESOL Journal, 10,* 137–143.

Wadden, P., & Hilke, R. (1999). Comments on Liz Hamp-Lyons' "Ethical test preparation practice: The case of the TOEFL": Polemic gone astray: A corrective to recent criticism of TOEFL preparation. *TESOL Quarterly, 33,* 263–270.

Warschauer, M. (2000). *Electronic literacies: Language, culture, and power in online education.* Mahwah, NJ: Lawrence Erlbaum Associates.

Wenden, A. L. (1992, February/March). Peace education: What and why? *TESOL Matters, 2,* 1, 6.

Wenden, A. L. (1995). Critical language education. In C. Schäffner & A. L. Wenden (Eds.), *Language and peace* (pp. 211–227). Aldershot, England: Dartmouth.

Young, I. M. (1990). *Justice and the politics of difference.* Princeton, NJ: Princeton University Press.

Zamel, V. (1997). Toward a model of transculturation. *TESOL Quarterly, 31,* 341–352.

Author Index

L

M

N

O-P

R

S

T

V-Z

Subject Index